IN THE REAR VIEW MIRROR
A Compilation

… In case you thought you saw it right the first time.

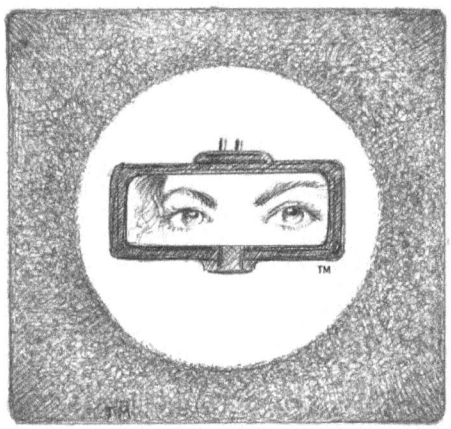

DK King and KAd Collins

EmPress DK Publications

No part of this publication may be reproduced or transmitted in any form or by any means, electronic or mechanical, including photocopy, recording or any information storage and retrieval system now known or to be invented without permission in writing from the publisher, except by a reviewer who wishes to quote brief passages in connection with a review written for inclusion in a magazine, newspaper, online article or broadcast.

Contact: EmPress DK Publications, Anaheim, CA.
Email: DKKingWriter@gmail.com

Book cover design by: Jaymie Lennon
Email: Jaymie.Lennon@gmail.com

Library of Congress Cataloging-in-Publication Data
King, DK and Collins, KAd
In The Rear View Mirror - A Compilation
ISBN: 978-0-9889744-2-5 (paperback)
Date of Publication: 1 September 2024

© by DK King and KAd Collins
All Rights Reserved.
Published by: EmPress DK Publications
www.DKKing.com

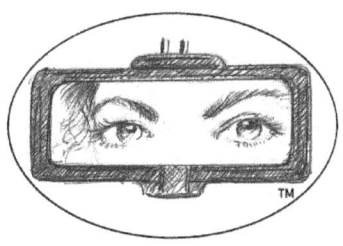

DK King dedicates this book to:
Kathie
For her enthusiastic support of this project from the start, and for being the beautiful sister that she was.

and

KAd Collins dedicates this book to:
Kristina
For expanding my world in ways I never thought possible.

IN THE REAR VIEW MIRROR
A Compilation

... In case you thought you saw it right the first time.

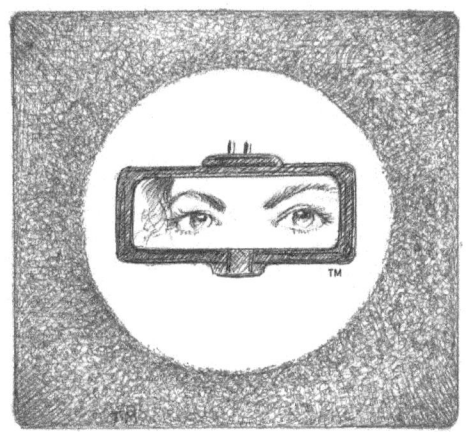

TABLE OF CONTENTS

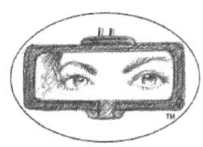

THE ROAD LESS TRAVELED BEGINS HERE 14

WELCOME ABOARD! AND DON'T FORGET YOUR SEATBELTS 25

ITRVM "W" BLOG SERIES 27

    WHIPLASHED OR BUSH-WHACKED? 28
    WHO WILL BE KING? 31
    WHO TOOK OFF WITH THE BANK? 34
    WILL THE REAL PIRATES PLEASE STAND UP? 37
    WHO ARE THE WIZARDS BEHIND THE TARP? 40
    WHITE HOUSE TENANT SERVED 60-DAY NOTICE TO VACATE 43
    WILL THEY GET DUBAI A STAIRWAY TO HEAVEN? 46
    WHO WILL DRIVE THE WILD CAR IN WASHINGTON? 49
    WHY BERNIE MADE OFF WITH 2008 52
    WHAT COMES IN 3'S? 55

ITRVM "W" DREAM SEQUENCES 59

    WALL STREET SCROOGES LIVE THE DREAM 60
    WHO'S BURNING BUSH? 61
    WILL THE LAME DUCK BE FLYING SOUTH FOR THE WINTER? 62
    WASHINGSTONE B.C. 65
    WORLD FORWARDS FINAL BILL TO "W" IN CRAWFORD, TX 68
    WHO'S TALKING LIKE A PIRATE NOW? 70
    WAS THAT WINGTIP A SIZE 10? 73
    WHAT HAPPENED TO MY OTHER HALF? 76
    SO LONG, FAREWELL, AUF WIEDERSEHEN, GOOD NIGHT 79

ITRVM BLOG SERIES 81

Taking The Bull By The Horns 82
Catching A Few Xe's 86
Big Brother Goes Hard ... Drive, That Is 88
Barbie, BFF 91
The American Myth 94
Greed Goes Underground 97
New Century Nurturing 101
The Boyling Point 104
Carnac The FMRI 107
The Sopranos Return For Another Season on HMO 110
Short Sighted 112
Mediocre Minds Think Alike 115
Wait Weight 118
Faux Food 121
Apple Pie Goes Rogue 125
Cashing In On COIN 129
Looking The Part 132
Seeing Double 135
POTUS, Inc. 137
Pomp and Promises 141
Trolling For Transparency 144
Dialing For Your Dollars 147
Bigger Than Life 150
T.S.A.: It's Our Business To Touch Yours 154
Walker's Waterloo 158
2012 - The Year Of The Job 161
The New GOP – Gender Overlord Party 162

ITRVM DREAM SEQUENCES 169

Camp Fed Takes The Triple 170
The Devil's In The Details 173
When Karma Comes Calling 176
The Salon Beyond 180
Ticker Trade 183
Reinczarnation 185
Rise Of The Global Republic 188
Casanova Works The Strip 191

THE ART OF REALITY 197
WALLED OFF 199
MOUNT OLYMPUS CHARIOT SALE 202
GREED TAKES A HOLIDAY 204
TEA HEE HAW 207
   Tea Hee Haw Sing Along..211
MORE MOVES TO DOMINATE THE WORLD 213
WHICH VIEW IS WITCH? 217
BILLZ ABOVE 221

ITRVM VICE VERSA VERSES...**225**
   WEDDED BIZ..226
ITRVM DICTIONARY **228**
ABOUT THE AUTHORS...**238**

THE ROAD LESS TRAVELED BEGINS HERE

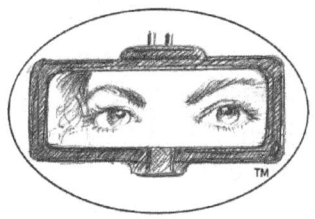

"**In The Rear View Mirror**" is a creative collaboration between KAd Collins (Artist/Intuitive) and myself (DK King, Writer) that evolved after more than two decades of lengthy phone conversations between longtime friends about our daily lives and the state of the world around us. Given the fact that the two of us were not living in the same part of the country during this time, the telephone, and later the cell phone, was logistically our preferred style of communication.

Our decision to take the road less traveled actually began a full year before the rubber met the road with the official creation of our "**InTheRearViewMirror.com**" blog in September, 2008. And it started with a typical phone conversation in September, 2007 when KAd exclaimed out of nowhere that Countrywide Home Loans was going to collapse.

WHAT? Countrywide collapse? How could Countrywide collapse when it was clearly one of the largest mortgage lenders in the nation at that time and essentially considered indomitable within the industry? It was an icon to many and believed to be too big to fail.

Since my professional career path was steeped in the real estate and mortgage banking industries, this warning about Countrywide admittedly put a big hiccup in my giddy up because I could immediately foresee the domino effect a collapse of this magnitude would create in not only the financial markets and real estate at large, but in my livelihood close to home.

Many in the lending business were fatly feeding off of the boom-time frenzy being reported to the general public during this timeframe. I, on the other hand, was already experiencing the tightening and it was a different kind of pinch. Change was in the air. I could feel it, and while my decades of industry experience had seen me through several rinse-and-repeat boom and bust cycles, nothing could quite prepare me for what was to come.

My first clue had arrived in April, 2007 when New Century Financial Corporation filed for bankruptcy. New Century Mortgage was a major subprime lender and the first big one to go bust without warning. But there were plenty of other large subprime lenders to fill its place so few took note. The bull market continued to expand the bubble as property values unsustainably inflated, interest rates dropped lower than ever before, and Wall Street's ravenous demand for collateralized portfolios filled with questionable subprime mortgage paper increased.

And then it happened. KAd was right as she so often is. Countrywide collapsed before the end of 2007 and the Global Financial Crisis of 2007-2008 officially began the "too big to fail" era. Economists and central bankers attempted to gloss over the magnitude of the bubble's eruption by referring to this era as "The Great Recession" instead of what it really was: a great reset.

"Ordo ab Chao[1]" was the force driving 2008 from what we could see. Financial chaos reigned and things were reorganizing so fast

---

[1] **ORDO AB CHAO**: A Latin expression meaning "Order out of Chaos." It is an important principle of the 33rd degree rooted in Scottish Rite Freemasonry.

that many couldn't see what was truly happening until it was too late.

Countrywide was only the beginning and before 2008 was over, we saw a very troubled Bank of America compelled into buying Countrywide and its toxic assets for +/- $40 Billion with the use of TARP[1] taxpayer bailout funds. Then we saw Bank of America coerced further into acquiring Merrill Lynch and its enormous deficit barely three months later, again with the use of taxpayer bailout funds.

We also saw Lehman Brothers become insolvent and dissolved in bankruptcy after 158 years in business. Next we saw AIG (American International Group, Inc.) begging Ben Bernanke, Chairman of the Federal Reserve central bank, for +/- $182 Billion in TARP bailout funds to prevent its collapse because the collapse of AIG would trigger a domino collapse of the numerous insurance and Wall Street firms it was linked to.

The grand finale for us, though, was the shocking arrest of Bernie Madoff in December, 2008 when the bottom fell out of his Wall Street investment pyramid scheme. He not only took down his very elite and exclusive international clientele with him, but his family as well.

---

[1] **TARP** (Troubled Asset Relief Program) is a direct result of the Emergency Economic Stabilization Act of October, 2008 (aka "Bank Bailout of 2008" and "Wall Street Bailout") enacted by President George W. Bush which allowed the U.S. government to use taxpayer funds to the tune of $700 Billion to purchase toxic assets and equity from failing banks/financial institutions in order to prop up and prevent a total financial sector collapse said to be due in part to the subprime mortgage crisis.

While the financial maneuverings of the "too big to fail" boys was happening on a grand scale and mostly behind closed doors, the casualties and losses on a local level were less reported although felt by most. We saw more banks, lenders and businesses than we can count become insolvent and close down as a direct result of the ensuing credit crunch. Apparently, at the heart of it all, was a greedy financial industry that saw no need to self-regulate (thank you, Bill Clinton).

The great reset we were witnessing felt less like the beneficial restructuring it was publicly hyped to be and more like a set up for another crisis in the future. As far as we could see, the reset was structured to temporarily patch the pig (or should we say, piggy bank?) while kicking the "checks and balances" can down the road.

Along with the financial chaos came the political chaos for 2008 was an election year to boot. Then current Republican President, George W. Bush, was finishing up his second term in office and was considered a lame duck president who appeared to have little to say in how the financial crisis was to be managed. We couldn't help but wonder if the Global Financial Crisis was designed to traumatize our economy the way 9-11 (September 11, 2001) was designed to traumatize our society – trauma events that both began and ended with his presidency.

The primary party candidates on the 2008 presidential ballot were John McCain (AZ)/Sarah Palin (AK), Republican; and Barack Obama (IL)/Joe Biden (DE), Democrat. Suffice to say, the year of 2008 was nothing more than a political circus to any observer.

Many of us know how fierce the political party rhetoric can get during election years in the United States, but 2008 was, in our opinion, a cross between kabuki theatre and WWE wrestling. The swinging of the favored party pendulum this particular year was casting heavy shade on the Republican GOP. This was evidently in preparation for a dominant party switchover in the November, 2008 election with the selection of Democrat, Barack Obama, who was basically a candidate that came out of nowhere.

Again, the whole thing was feeling like a set up for a repeat performance down the road, except now there would be a new cast and crew.

Now KAd and I are not politically motivated people overall, primarily because we tend to see the 2-party political system of this country as two sides of the same coin – each party presenting what appears to be opposing platforms and agendas in order to create divisions within society while compelling people to pick one side against the other and each other. All said, still the same coin. And frankly, we wanted to know who minted, owned, and controlled the whole coin.

In the labeling of things and people, we would generally be classified as belonging to the Baby Boomer generation. We have observed and experienced great changes within our lifetimes and we take the old saying, "He who doesn't know history is doomed to repeat it," quite seriously because using the past in the present to project the future down the road is what "**In The Rear View Mirror**" is predicated on.

We have also come to recognize that it is our responsibility to know what our history is. Our real history, and not the distorted lies passed off as history as taught in our highly deficient national school system. If we really wanted to know the truth about our world and its control structure, it was clear we needed to open our minds beyond the limits of our school system indoctrination and become autodidactic.

Thankfully, autodidacticism came naturally for us both since we are highly observant, curious and love to learn. Yet, to better understand the chaos happening around us that was, for all intents and purposes our history in the making, we realized that we needed to start asking different questions. This is why we chose to end our "**In The Rear View Mirror**" narratives with a question worth ruminating.

So what motivated us to create the blog when we did?

First let me say that in 2008 social media platforms like Facebook and Twitter (now "X") were still in their early stages, and YouTube was relatively new as well. For us, creating a blog simply felt like the best platform available at the time to share what we wanted to share without getting overly complicated.

This does not mean that we didn't utilize Facebook and Twitter for exposure and promotion because we did. In fact, we had more than 8,000 followers on Facebook in 2009 before "they" shut down our accounts overnight without warning, never to be accessed again. It took us a while to figure out what had happened and why, and it boiled down to censorship. Censorship before anyone thought censorship was a thing on these new platforms promoting freedom of speech and the like.

We later came to understand that our Facebook accounts were closed down by the FB censorship police no one knew existed not long after we posted a "Dream Sequence[1]" titled "Ticker Trade" on August 7, 2009. Without fully realizing it at the time, we had

---

[1] **DREAM SEQUENCE:** An ITRVM Allegory where we weave things together that don't seem to go together to create a vision of things to come. We liken these to random, off-road detours along the lookout ledge of our own private Idaho. We also like to call these "Crazy Ivans."

dropped a truth bomb that "they" apparently didn't want gaining traction.

And our "Ticker Trade" post didn't just get noticed by the FB censorship police, but parts of it unquestionably showed up in an opening monologue delivered by Stephen Colbert of "The Colbert Report" one evening shortly after it was posted.

The motivation to create our blog in September, 2008 was catalyzed by several things, and of course, the Global Financial Crisis and ensuing chaos was a big part of it. Our initial drive, however, had everything to do with the public presentation of George W. Bush (or "W," as he was often called) and his chronic blunders during an 8-year term as President that began with 9-11 and ended with the Global Financial Crisis.

It made us laugh every time we thought about "W's" first day in the Oval Office back in January, 2001 when he replaced Bill Clinton as Head of State knowing that the departing Clinton administration staffers had pranked "W's" new administration by removing the "W" keys from many of the computer keyboards in the Old Executive Building in the White House, thereby removing access to the new president's middle initial and nickname. This prank was the inspiration behind our "**W**" Headliner Series in which every story and Dream Sequence headline ceremoniously began with the letter "**W**" until he left office.

Most would agree that laughter is a special kind of medicine, especially when things around us feel scary and uncertain.

The late night pundits figured this out long ago and have used laughter nightly to distract the masses by poking fun at the chaos and fear most especially felt by a disintegrating middle class. Today the pundits are still working hard at this disempowering distraction game as they remodel the negative news into a comedy routine so we can laugh at the darkness happening around us in a disconnected way, lapse into overwhelm and helpless complacency, and hopefully, forget about the rest.

Fortunately, KAd and I have a similar, and somewhat dry, twisty sense of humor. We've often attributed this to our Irish roots and the born ability to relieve inner stress by taking what is uncomfortable or frightening and becoming empowered by finding the funny or absurd in it. Some would call that seeing the other side of a situation.

Constructively finding humor in the hard truths and fearful things that hold power over us is also a well-known way of raising one's frequency from the inevitable dis-ease we all contend with in a highly toxic world. When we raise our emotional vibration with genuine mirth, our fear-based perceptions can't help but shift for the better with the increased frequency. This frequency shift can be further amplified when we develop an inner wisdom and knowledge base that has been cultivated through personal research and introspection.

We may not be able to change the world at large but we can change how we perceive and respond to it, thereby consciously changing our reality and the environment around us.

Along with our compatible senses of humor, we are also highly intuitive; KAd exceptionally so. This extra-sensory aspect has allowed us to weave added layers of multi-dimensionality into our narratives that may not be evident at first glance. We feel there is enjoyment to be had whether the reader approaches our stories from a current events-linear layer (3rd dimensional), from a secret societies-hidden mysteries-occult layer (4th dimensional), or from an expanded awareness-spiritual layer (5th dimensional). There is validity in all of it.

In the end, what is perceived will all depend on the reader's level of awareness and ability to read between the lines because our stories are visionary and futuristic, with messages scattered throughout in the form of double entendres, metaphors and a between-the-lines symbolism. So you might want to pay attention, or even read them again … in case you thought you saw it right the first time.

On a wider scope, our narratives are ultimately devised to inspire introspection regarding the many dualities we have interwoven within our present reality and the part we want to play in changing this reality for the betterment of all.

But what we really want to know is how much has actually changed on the world stage since 2008 other than the actors on the stage?

DK King
July, 2024

DISCLAIMER

"**In The Rear View Mirror**" is a creative collaboration between **DK King** (Writer) and **KAd Collins** (Artist/Intuitive) that offers up an ironic parody of the obvious and absurd as seen through collective eyes. The anecdotes we have written here are clearly our perceptions of life on the ground and current events during this profound, yet chaotic time known to the sensitive as humanity's "Great Awakening."

Our narratives are for the mind-altering entertainment of our readers. For those experiencing cognitive dissonance (or as we like to put it: For those standing in a blind spot), we encourage the pursuit of expanded awareness through personal research and reflection.

Welcome aboard and enjoy the ride!

Welcome Aboard! And Don't Forget Your Seatbelts
September 15, 2008

Let's face it. Things are looking pretty scary out there and the media isn't bringing peace of mind to the world. It's times like these that make late night comedians a primary news source for more of the population than CNN may like to admit since humor seems to be the most palatable way for the everyday human to digest it all without falling apart.

This blog is an evolution of more than two decades of lengthy phone conversations – especially given the fact that the two of us haven't even lived in the same state since the late 1980's and thankfully, Verizon has an in-calling plan – about philosophy, current events, the past-the present-the future, and the state of the world at large through the filters of our personal experiences and our independent (and quite unrelated) professional disciplines.

Throughout the decades, we have shared many personal changes of the usual and unusual kind: marriages, children, divorces, deaths, parental challenges, financial duress (including the loss of our 401Ks); and we believe our unique interpretations may offer slanted insight and perhaps a different approach to these historic economic times.

What we know about ourselves is that we are risk takers. We are masters of observation and we are visionaries. We are ahead of things in one blink and then stop to scratch our heads because it seems we've been left behind in the next. We call that gas and brakes. We have a similar and somewhat dry, twisty sense of humor which has proven essential to our mental and emotional survival. And we believe that most of us do the very best we can each and every day.

We invite you to ride along with us as we give you our visions from **the rear view mirror**, and of course, from the **side mirrors** on occasion.

DK and KAd

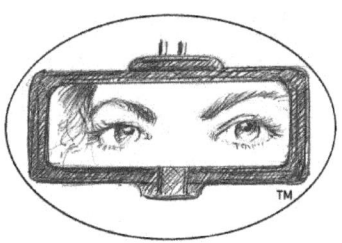

ITRVM "W" Blog Series

1

Whiplashed or Bush-Whacked?
September 20, 2008

Wow! What a week!!

Driving down our free-market super highway (which has been predictably constructed for over 200 years), we hit a sink-hole that rocked our world, blew out a tire, cracked our windshield and took us over the edge into financial darkness. We barely had a chance to glance **in the rear view mirror** as we were going down.

At this point, we found it necessary to get out of the car to assess the damage, and there was no Bernanke[1] Towing Service or Bail-Me-Out Bond in sight.

So now what? We're sitting on the side of the road, with not a Thomas Jefferson nickel to our name (maybe because 3.5 million of them were spilled across the highway in a rollover pile-up in Bush brother Jeb's state of mind, aka Florida), to ponder how on Earth did this happen to our "Wild West" capitalistic approach to world economics?

Given the frantic pace with which our old world economy is dying, it's obvious we won't be able to hang around too long on the side of this road because while it may be promised, it doesn't appear that anyone will be along any time soon to bail us out. Not really, even though we thought we had insurance coverage for all

---

[1] **BENNY**: Federal Reserve Bank Chairman, Ben S. Bernanke, appointed by President George W. Bush and sworn in February 1, 2006. He was the successor to Alan Greenspan at a time when Atlas Shrugged, and he became 2008's crowned Cannibal King after running Hank (aka Henry S. Paulson, Jr.) off the road.

of this. It seems the best option right now would be to just get out the jack, change our own tire, and get limping on down the road – doughnut tire, shattered windshield and all.

The windshield was cracked in two which makes us believe that we have definitely come to a fork in the road. Do we go left, or do we go right?

Looking **in the rear view mirror**, we can certainly see the global Red Shield's[1] trend-setting re-positioning, and the overall direction moving toward privatizing profit and socializing liability. We wondered, "Has this been the plan all along?" The bigger question still is what larger, long-term, and all-encompassing international strategy is moving into place?

Looking to the right, what do we see? We see a probable reconstruction of major portions of the free-market super highway with perhaps a new bridge (some would call this economic re-shuffling) allowing the MOWBs[2] to continue to run the world on our tank of gas, and with our permission no less, over the next +4 years.

Looking to the left, what do we see? We see the probable dissemination and/or restructuring of the banking mystery known as the Federal Reserve within the next +3 years into more

---

[1] **RED SHIELD**: The Rothschild Banking Family.
[2] **MOLDY OLD WHITE BREAD, or "MOWB"** (Archetype): A tasty depiction of a human anachronism who routinely derives sustenance from stale, inedible, and moldy ways of thinking, while advocating modus operandi that is firmly entrenched in standards set by the "Old Guard." MOWBs are not conservatively categorized or necessarily stereotyped by gender, age, race, culture, or even political party affiliation; but usually reveal their unmistakable MOWB-ness with a mindset deeply rooted in entitlement, arrogance, superiority and double standards.

transparent and separately managed sectors, thus providing us with a healthier "checks and balances" atmosphere.

What will you invest in and which direction will you choose to avoid being "Bush-Whacked[1]?"

---

[1] **BUSH-WHACKED:** 1) We play and you get to pay. 2) Shootin' from the hip into dead space and living with the consequences of someone else's good idea for you that has essentially no basis in reality, no vision, no foresight. You know, like a bad blind date that goes nowhere fast, and yet somehow, you're left holding the check. 3) 21st Century synonym for "it's my way or the highway." 4) Cronyism.

2

Who Will Be King?
September 26, 2008

The financial winter storm has arrived early this century and here we sit, alone and exposed, on the side of the road with not even a mink coat to keep us warm.

Tire jack in hand, we finally pulled out the Bear Stearns doughnut tire and made that change to our front passenger-side flat without assistance. OK, done. Now it's time to hobble slowly back onto the free-market economic super highway and try to navigate Washington D.C.'s new 2-lane Donner Pass, when what do we see **in the rear view mirror**, coming up from behind and seemingly out of nowhere? Two large white vehicles fast approaching at lightning speed; each driver blindly focused on its hot pursuit of the other and clearly oblivious to us or their surroundings.

Our heads spin as if Daddy Warbucks[1] was spending his last $5 Billion while we watch the White SUV zoom past us on the left leaving the White Minivan[2] jammed up behind us. Imagine our

---

[1] **DADDY WARBUCKS**: Warren E. Buffett, CEO of Berkshire Hathaway, who has been considered at times to be the richest man in the world. AKA the fox put in charge of the chicken coop, and the inspiration for The BIG BOPR's (aka Barack Obama) "Buffett Rule." Although Daddy Warbucks won't officially endorse his namesake "Buffett Rule," we'll always remember that he was the slyest fox of all by suggesting that all the other rich foxes pay a proper tax.

[2] **WHITE MINIVAN** (Theory): This is a theory which basically asserts that nothing good ever comes from a White Minivan. When you notice that the flow of traffic is inexplicably interrupted, just look ahead, and discover for yourself that invariably the source of the hold-up is a White Minivan. Examples demonstrate it best: 1. Stopped in the carpool lane while the cars in every other lane whoosh by with the speed of light? Try to look beyond the gigantic SUV in front of you and see who's at the head of the line – bet it's a White Minivan. 2. Have you ever found yourself humming with the flow of freeway traffic when out of nowhere comes that White Minivan from the fast lane who's just realized

surprise to see Bernanke, at the helm of the White SUV, swerve vigorously to block the side-swiping maneuver of Paulson in the White Minivan. Although Benny[1] appeared to be confident about his lead in this amazing race, Hank's[2] face too reflected a distinct mask of determined victory. We were trapped in the middle and afraid for our future, afraid for our lives. Before eating their dust entirely, we had to pull over once again, this time to catch our breath.

In a state of complete disbelief at the steeplechase we've just witnessed, we feel compelled to ask the very question one would ask when the unbelievable has just occurred, "What could possibly be in our blind spot that we don't see coming?"

A casual backward glance **in the rear view mirror** gives us a glimpse of another time, long, long ago … back to the Salem

---

it's about to miss the off-ramp it needs in an 1/8th of a mile, as you speechlessly witness it cut off all 4 lanes of traffic (including your own and the semi's) just in time to make that exit, and with 1/16th of a mile to spare?   3. Stopped at a signal, sandwiched in with mouth agape, when the White Minivan in front of you backs up straight into your front bumper with its projecting trailer hitch (leaving a very un-aerodynamic hole in its wake) because it didn't think anyone was behind it and it wanted to turn around without driving around the block? (And yes, we have had this happen). Get the idea? Our observational research thus far supports the belief that this theory applies to large White Vans and most White SUVs as well. **Side Mirror** Footnote: White Minivans typically run in packs with other minivans, and they tend to herd or congregate around school parking lots and the shopping centers of suburbia. These suburban parking lot gatherings take on a surreal life of their own (not far from Stepford) in an asphalt dimension called the "Land of the Minivan."

[1] **BENNY**: Federal Reserve Bank Chairman, Ben S. Bernanke, appointed by President George W. Bush and sworn in February 1, 2006. He was the successor to Alan Greenspan at a time when Atlas Shrugged, and he became 2008's crowned Cannibal King after running Hank (aka Henry S. Paulson, Jr.) off the road.

[2] **HANK**: 74th Secretary of the Treasury, Henry S. Paulson, Jr., nominated by President George W. Bush in June, 2006. He was the former Chairman and CEO of Goldman Sachs. AKA the 2008 Cannibal King contender who was overtaken by Benny (aka Ben S. Bernanke) and swiftly ran off the road, but at least he managed to save Goldman Sachs after the crash.

witch hunt days of the 1690's when the stored rye crop used for making the community's bread developed mold, and those who consumed the bread it produced began hallucinating. In the acid-trip-like psychosis and subsequent hysteria that ensued, accusations began to fly and innocent bodies burned.

Snapping our attention back to today, we never cease to be surprised at how history repeats itself because we're seeing it happen all over again. Except this time, the Moldy Old White Breads[1] have begun eating each other alive causing similar mold-induced hallucinations. They're seeing illusions in their **side view mirrors** that only their fervent elite supporters can see; fingers are pointing and accusations are flying.

What innocents will be burned at the stake while the two (appointed, but not elected) Cannibals decide who will be King?

---

[1] **MOLDY OLD WHITE BREAD, or "MOWB"** (Archetype): A tasty depiction of a human anachronism who routinely derives sustenance from stale, inedible, and moldy ways of thinking, while advocating modus operandi that is firmly entrenched in standards set by the "Old Guard." MOWBs are not conservatively categorized or necessarily stereotyped by gender, age, race, culture, or even political party affiliation; but usually reveal their unmistakable MOWB-ness with a mindset deeply rooted in entitlement, arrogance, superiority and double standards.

3

Who Took Off With The Bank?
October 1, 2008

Whew! We just barely missed getting all tangled up in 700 tons of racing White Minivans[1] and we're back on the road. We admit, we're feeling and looking pretty dilapidated right now as we push our gimpy selves further along Washington D.C.'s Donner Pass. But we've side-stepped a mighty large collision and we're feeling a little lucky about it.

Chugging onward and upward, determined to reach the apex of the Pass, nothing could've astounded us more than to see four lonely boys looking like versions of Huckleberry Finn standing on the side of the road trying to hitch a ride to the top.

Three of the boys stood together holding a large sign that read, "BAIL US OUT," while the fourth stood nearby clutching a large piggy bank in his right arm like a football. We couldn't resist the rescue attempt.

They announced themselves while climbing into our back seat. The biggest boy, and the first to get into our car, was "Bad Assets.[2]" Next was "ChaseURMoney[3]," followed by "Won't Go Far[4]," and lastly, "CitiGombeens[5]."

---

[1] **WHITE MINIVAN** (Theory): See "Dictionary" for full description and definition.
[2] **Bad Assets**: Bank of America.
[3] **ChaseURMoney**: Chase Bank.
[4] **Won't Go Far**: Wells Fargo Bank.
[5] **CitiGombeens**: CitiBank.

Taking pity on their sorry state, we threw them a quarter in the back. We watched those boys **in the rear view mirror** fight over that quarter as it flew about, slipping between each of their hands like a hot potato, before the biggest boy in the back, Bad Assets, decisively secured the coin.

He quickly inserted the quarter into the piggy bank's slot and that's when it all began … the piggy's red eyes lit up and started to spin back into its head as the curly tail whirled around and smoke blew out of the hole beneath it. Yikes! That piggy swiftly grew hungry fangs and squealed out a nursery rhyme we'd never heard before to the tune of "Three Blind Mice:"

Four once united, four now divided
See the money grow, see now what they sow
They won the world in monopoly,
And hid their sins in philanthropy
The Red Shield's[1] call, "Integrity for All!!"

Finally nearing the highway's pinnacle and looming right before us, D.C.'s Donner Pass was abruptly dissected by an intersection completely overshadowed by the sun-blocking silhouettes of four of the world's tallest buildings, one standing on each corner. They blocked out the sunlight like the ninth plague.

As we tried to move forward, our car unbelievably stalled right in the middle of the intersection, right in the middle of the darkness. None of this seemed to faze the four boys in our backseat, however, who collectively shrieked, "We're Home!" And without so much as a thank you or backward glance, those four boys spun out of our car like a pinwheel, each whirligigging toward a different corner and its own respective Big House.

---

[1] **RED SHIELD**: The Rothschild Banking Family.

The problem is, as we sat there in the dark, we never saw who took the piggy bank. Did you?

4

Will The Real Pirates Please Stand Up?
October 8, 2008

Stalled in the middle of the intersection as if we'd run out of gas, we sat alone in the dark, with no true illumination from D.C. to show us the way. Or so we thought, until we heard the thundering jet engines of Air Force One oscillate above us. We looked up, high in the sky, and witnessed a breathtaking sight.

Out of Air Force One's rear passenger door, and atop the discharged emergency evacuation slide that flapped spastically in the air, spewed forth all of the financial district's CEOs with golden parachutes strapped to their backs. Their parachutes glittered in the style of fool's gold.

Although they fell toward the ground in droves (and randomly like care packages that are dropped into POW camps when any war is nearing an end), we tried to follow each parachute as it opened up and released what we later learned was a new viral strain formally classified as the "Bush Flu[1]." Subsequent studies eventually confirmed that the virus was carried and transmitted through the small air-borne drops of crude oil that leeched from the edges of the parachutes upon deployment.

---

[1] **BUSH FLU:** A highly resistant and uncooperative viral strain that was released from the golden parachutes strapped to the backs of financial district CEOs as they were ejected by their Board of Directors and pushed out of Air Force One. Subsequent studies eventually confirmed that the virus was carried and transmitted through the small air-borne drops of crude oil that leeched from the edges of the golden parachutes upon deployment. Symptoms include: Great Depression. No money in the bank. Your bank's ATM machine holds your debit card hostage and instead spits out a government I.O.U. by way of a receipt in the form of Federal Reserve Notes.

It became evident almost immediately that a majority of those golden parachutes were never going to hit the ground, let alone make it down safely. Out of nowhere appeared several old hand-me-down helicopters from a third world country that began to ominously encircle Air Force One. It was difficult to distinguish the origin of these helicopters because the only identifying marks they had were matching mission statements hastily spray-painted onto their side panels that simply read, "WE'RE IN IT FOR THE MONEY."

From the choppers' opened side doors emerged a countless outpouring of Somalian hang-gliders, and we watched in amazement as they swooped in and intercepted nearly all of the golden parachutes after ejection from Air Force One.

From our vantage point in the middle of the intersection, we could see a few of the CEOs slip through the swarm of hang-gliding pirates and hit the ground around us. And **in the rear view mirror** we witnessed a duplicitous spectacle when a swarm of attorneys came running from all directions, clawing over each other as they scurried out to meet-n-greet the fallen CEOs like ambulance chasers.

Regrettably, a large portion of the CEOs were seized mid-air by the Somalian Pirates[1] because, well, we could state the obvious in saying that "like attracts like," but the truth of the matter is, they didn't even know they were high-jacking golden parachutes. They really thought they were getting $700 Billion[2] in subprime

---

[1] **SOMALIAN PIRATES**: The Somali Pirates and their highly lucrative ransom demands were a major threat to international shipping and boating off the Somalian peninsula/Horn of Africa during the war in Somalia from 2006 to 2009. Somalia was considered a failed state until 2012.

[2] **TARP** (Troubled Asset Relief Program) is a direct result of the Emergency Economic Stabilization Act of October, 2008 (aka "Bank Bailout of 2008" and "Wall Street Bailout") enacted by President George W. Bush which allowed the

mortgage paper that they could convert into quick cash on the secondary market.

If all that glitters isn't gold (and that includes black gold), then who will survive, or perhaps even build an immunity to, the coming "Bush Flu" season?

U.S. government to use taxpayer funds to the tune of $700 Billion to purchase toxic assets and equity from failing banks/financial institutions in order to prop up and prevent a total financial sector collapse said to be due in part to the subprime mortgage crisis.

5

Who Are The Wizards Behind The TARP?
October 23, 2008

It seems that ejecting the financial district's golden parachute-packing CEOs from Air Force One just wasn't enough. We gasped when we caught sight of the final package to be thrown out of the rear door before the jet sped off like an F-22 Raptor.

The grand finale was a massive Hot Air Balloon, airbrushed in its entirety with a larger-than-life image of King George looking like a madman. The regal banner underneath his portrait read, "Everything is going to be fine."

Looking up, we stared directly into the frightened eyes of an 8-year old girl in pig tails as she peered over the side of the balloon's basket while holding on to her little dog named RoveR[1]. She tried not to panic when the hot air-producing flame which fed the balloon's enormous cavity started to sputter then fizzle out, and the (not-so-hot-air) balloon commenced to free fall.

In our rear view mirror we kept constant tabs on the speedy approach of the two Cannibal King racing minivans we thought we'd lost way back on D.C.'s Donner Pass. We cringed when both drivers eventually slammed on their brakes too close on our tail

---

[1] **RoveR**: Karl Rove was known to be a Republican political consultant, policy advisor and lobbyist in his role as Senior Advisor and Deputy Chief of Staff during the administration of President George W. Bush, resigning this role in August, 2007. Rove vigorously defended the Bush administration's use of torture known as waterboarding. He founded "American Crossroads" in 2010, a U.S. Super PAC that raises funds from "secret" donors to advocate for certain chosen Republican candidates. American Crossroads devised many new methods of corporate fundraising that were opened up by the Supreme Court's "Citizens United" ruling.

for comfort. Brakes screeched, rubber burned, back tires peeled then skid, and road stones spewed in every direction upon their dramatic, simultaneous finish right beside us.

There sat Benny[1] at the helm of his White SUV, and by the looks of it, he'd picked up a solitary companion along the way. Sitting in the front passenger seat was a scarecrow[2] tightly clutching a paperback of "Atlas Shrugged."

Hank[3], on the other hand, had stuffed his White Minivan[4] to overflowing. In the front passenger seat was VP Dick Cheney holding a shotgun and dripping with the scent of road-kill. The back of the minivan was packed with Hank's Goldman Sachs fraternity bros plus his most recent pickup, Daddy Warbucks[5]. Like a bunch of back seat drivers, the riders in his minivan were all screaming to be heard at the same time, each with different advise and its own personal opinion of which way the minivan

---

[1] **BENNY**: Federal Reserve Bank Chairman, Ben S. Bernanke, appointed by President George W. Bush and sworn in February 1, 2006. He was the successor to Alan Greenspan at a time when Atlas Shrugged, and he became 2008's crowned Cannibal King after running Hank (aka Henry S. Paulson, Jr.) off the road.

[2] **ALAN GREENSPAN**: Greenspan was a former chairman of the Federal Reserve Bank Board from 1987 to 2006. He was a known Ayn Rand proselyte and committed "Atlas Shrugged" fan who routinely carried a paperback version of the book around on his person.

[3] **HANK**: 74th Secretary of the Treasury, Henry S. Paulson, Jr., nominated by President George W. Bush in June, 2006. He was the former Chairman and CEO of Goldman Sachs. AKA the 2008 Cannibal King contender who was overtaken by Benny (aka Ben S. Bernanke) and swiftly ran off the road, but at least he managed to save Goldman Sachs after the crash.

[4] **WHITE MINIVAN** (Theory): See "Dictionary" for full description and definition.

[5] **DADDY WARBUCKS**: Warren E. Buffett, CEO of Berkshire Hathaway, who has been considered at times to be the richest man in the world. AKA the fox put in charge of the chicken coop, and the inspiration for The BIG BOPR's (aka Barack Obama) "Buffett Rule." Although Daddy Warbucks won't officially endorse his namesake "Buffett Rule," we'll always remember that he was the slyest fox of all by suggesting that all the other rich foxes pay a proper tax.

needed to go. Except Daddy Warbucks, who just smiled like a fox put in charge of the chicken coop.

The Hot Air Balloon crash-landed directly in front of us. Benny, Hank and all of their ride-along buddies (even Daddy Warbucks) exploded from the two white vehicles and ran to the little girl. It looked as if they were rushing to her rescue, but all they did was snatch the ruby slippers right off of her feet and sprint back to their respective vehicles, patting each other on the back and smiling with smug satisfaction.

Unfortunately the dog, RoveR, did what dogs do best and what came naturally. It leaped out of the little girl's arms as the shoes were being ripped from her very feet because it was time to find something to lift its leg on. And Cheney's own shoe, smelling of road kill, was the perfect target. Business done, the dog pranced off. But it didn't get far, however. Cheney is a pretty good shot.

Reeling from this shocking display, we wondered who's going to save the little girl now? Oui. Oui.

6

White House Tenant Served 60-Day Notice To Vacate
November 7, 2008

It's high noon. A trickle of light from the sun has finally begun to seep through and even though we've been stalled in the middle of this intersection for what seems like an eternity, we no longer harbor a sense of being abandoned on the dark side of the moon.

Yes, we've witnessed some incredibly dramatic events unfold as we sat immobilized at the pinnacle of D.C.'s Donner Pass. And true, we're not for the moment any better off than we were when our car first stalled, but at least the ignition started this time when we turned the key. Moving through and out of this impasse, we can, for a short spell anyway, coast our way downhill into the nation's capital.

When we arrived at 1600 Pennsylvania Avenue, we stopped to read the legal notice conspicuously posted for public viewing on the front fence. It was a 60-day Notice to Vacate. Looks like XP "W"[1]'s second 4-year lease term on the White House is up, and he's been ordered out.

No sooner had "W" been formally served with his 60-day Notice, when the film crews began showing up at his door and they weren't there for him. Seemed he was now out of the loop, and no one thought to tell him that the White House had just been selected the new winner of an "Extreme Makeover-Home

---

[1] **XP "W"**: Ex-President George W. Bush, 43rd President of the United States of America, Inc., officially sworn in to office January 20, 2001. He served two disastrous 4-year terms then finally crashed and burned his way out on January 19, 2009. He was succeeded by The Big BOPR (aka Barack Obama).

Edition." When Ty Pennington appeared unannounced with his pros to measure for new drapes and furnishings, and then the "Queer Eye" ensemble popped in to begin their work of designing the new occupant's flair (china, crystal, silverware, color schemes and seating arrangements) – and all of this without cost to the taxpayers – it was simply too much for a man of his stature to bear.

George immediately got Condi[1] on the phone and secretly arranged a protest rally to take place on the White House lawn. Some would accuse him of being too inebriated to remember much of the 1960's, but he was sure they used to do something like that back then, didn't they?

Well, instead of picketing for change, the protesters he was calling to action on what was still his front yard would be picketing for things to remain the same. It had been a good ride, and he couldn't just stand by and watch helplessly as his heady error (or was that era?) of the last 8 years abruptly ended.

When George's protest rally finally began that warm late fall morning (really it was more like afternoon when tee-times were over), we could see **in the rear view mirror** that it was a far cry from what had happened back in the '60's when the lines of rickety buses would pour into Washington D.C. from every corner of the country and unload at the White House gates an endless stream of pot smoking, flag burning hippies wearing tied-dye, flashing the peace sign and crying out for U.S. withdrawal from Vietnam, equal rights, free love and above all, change.

---

[1] **CONDI**: Condoleeza Rice, U.S. Secretary of State from 2005 to 2009 serving under the George W. Bush administration.

Fall afternoon 2008, Pennsylvania Avenue instead saw a line-up of Rolls Royce limousines, with a few Mercedes and Lincolns thrown in for good measure, far more impressive than any formal White House affair he'd ever hosted during his 8-year reign. One by one, the limos unloaded its Moldy Old White Bread[1] sporting tailored Armani suits and Rolex watches, well-fed on the caviar and Dom Perignon that had been elegantly served to them as they reposed in the backseat and waited for an opportunity to emerge from their transports.

Once the MOWBs were properly assembled, they began to clamor in unison for U.S. extension in Iraq (the oil revenues were just too good to give up, oh duh), more bail out money to pay their executive bonuses, and above all, keeping the Old Guard.

When "W's" rally is finally over, will the heads of the protesters continue spinning in drunken power, or will their heads be splitting in pain as they endure the inevitable champagne hangover?

---

[1] **MOLDY OLD WHITE BREAD, or "MOWB"** (Archetype): A tasty depiction of a human anachronism who routinely derives sustenance from stale, inedible, and moldy ways of thinking, while advocating modus operandi that is firmly entrenched in standards set by the "Old Guard." MOWBs are not conservatively categorized or necessarily stereotyped by gender, age, race, culture, or even political party affiliation; but usually reveal their unmistakable MOWB-ness with a mindset deeply rooted in entitlement, arrogance, superiority and double standards.

7

Will They Get Dubai A Stairway To Heaven?
November 22, 2008

XP "W"[1]'s White House lawn hullabaloo protesting the demise of the Old Guard was indeed an attention getter, but not enough to deter us from watching the super-sonic approach of three private jets **in our rear view mirror** preparing to land at The Gipper's Airport. The three jets zoomed over our heads in a pattern similar to that of migrating albatrosses looking for a rich ocean to feed in.

It's no mystery that the Big Three Automakers have been relentlessly petitioning Congress to throw them a $25 Billion bone. In the big scheme of things, it appears they may have come barking a little too late. And everybody knows timing is everything.

Well, it just wasn't the time to consider the pros and cons of effective timing because now that Congress had finally agreed to hear their supplications, there was no time to waste in making the appropriate D.C. travel arrangements for the big audience. As we sat nearby, it was easy to overhear a group of their executive assistants discussing the various travel possibilities that had been considered just days before.

CAR CARAVAN:
This would involve a scenic road trip from Detroit to D.C. in their biggest, newest, and most deluxe gas guzzling '09 models fresh off the assembly line floor. We quickly realized that by going this

---

[1] **XP "W"**: Ex-President George W. Bush, 43rd President of the United States of America, Inc., officially sworn in to office January 20, 2001. He served two disastrous 4-year terms then finally crashed and burned his way out on January 19, 2009. He was succeeded by The Big BOPR (aka Barack Obama).

route, they could've effectively promoted the very products they were in D.C. to represent by proudly parking them out in front of the Capital Building for everyone to see. All of this, along with a savvy sales team placed curbside to distribute attractive marketing brochures and offer seductive sales pitches, who knows? A sale or two may have even been made. Frankly, it was too much like driving to Florida or Seattle for the weekend. Option: Rejected!!

GREYHOUND BUS:
This was worse than Car Caravanning and not only that, travel like the working man? Option: Rejected!!

AMERICAN AIRLINES:
This would involve standing in a long line to get through airport security checkpoints which further meant they'd have to take off their tap shoes. And there again, travel like the working man? Option: Rejected!!

BLIMP-POOLING:
As a vision of the Hindenburg's 1937 1-minute incineration loomed before them, this option was promptly nixed. That rejection, however, did not come before they briefly considered that a little promo for Goodyear might not be a bad marketing ploy. There might've been a free ride in it for them as well. In the end, it seemed obvious to us that if they weren't inclined to promote their own products, then why would they promote the maker of the tires their vehicles ran upon? Free ride or no. Option: Rejected!!

PRIVATE JETS:
Fast, luxurious, equivalent to their elite status and everyone had their very own so no one had to share. Option: The Winner!!

When the Big Three Auto execs arrived at court, we got a **rear view mirror** flashback to the roaring '20's. The Big Three were walking anachronisms, dressed in the very clothes of their ancestors ... Tuxedos with bow ties, top hats, tap shoes, and the prerequisite solid gold pocket watches. Wafting invisibly through the airwaves was the tune "Puttin' on the Ritz."

We watched as GM CEO Richie Rick pulled out his pocket watch to check the time. The pressure he was under was interminable, and this included a stringent timeline – Richie Rick was due to be in Dubai in several days. As he retrieved the solid gold watch from his pocket, he failed to notice the invitation that popped out and fell to the ground beneath his fast dancing feet. It was an invitation to the party of the decade at the new hotel Atlantis on The Palm. We could see he wasn't too sure at this point whether he'd be celebrating with his tribe in Dubai or crying in his cups as he postured for an Arabian handout.

As the Big Three moved toward the inner chamber to settle in for some serious begging, they were surprised to see not 3 chairs, but only 2, placed out before the open court. And they logically wondered which one of them wouldn't get to sit in a chair. They didn't have to wonder long because Congressman Ackerman (D-NY) quickly hit a switch and Led Zeppelin's never-ending song, "Stairway to Heaven," began to play through the auditorium loud speakers. The three CEOs instinctively began a rapid tap dance around the 2 chairs as they each vied to be in a sitting position when the music stopped.

It was a tap dance that lasted two days, and while they pleaded for the music to stop, the music never did stop. When the music finally does stop, who will get to sit in a chair?

8

Who Will Drive The Wild Car in Washington?
December 14, 2008

Much to the chagrin of the Big Three Auto Titans, the music still hasn't stopped and their bronze medal dancing has tangoed on for weeks around very wobbly court chairs. What had started out as a respectable pleading, now had them retching humble pie on Mr. Toad's Wild Ride.

And what had started out as $25 Billion, had now been whittled down for the umteenth time to around $14 Billion. It was an eye-opening sight to behold the new King's court making its decisive motion to silence the music. Yet, just as the new King's court moved in to halt the Auto Titans' dance long enough for a sit-down, the old King's court hotfooted in posthaste and ripped the chairs right out from under everyone just because they could.

We could see **in our rear view mirror** that the ancient rituals of old court vs. new court would certainly not be changing this time around. Out of all this posturing, however, did emerge what appeared to be an unusually constructive solution to the Big Three's serious financial dilemma.

The Big Three Automakers would never see a dime ... from TARP[1] that is. Instead, Congress surprisingly agreed to take the

---

[1] **TARP** (Troubled Asset Relief Program) is a direct result of the Emergency Economic Stabilization Act of October, 2008 (aka "Bank Bailout of 2008" and "Wall Street Bailout") enacted by President George W. Bush which allowed the U.S. government to use taxpayer funds to the tune of $700 Billion to purchase toxic assets and equity from failing banks/financial institutions in order to prop up and prevent a total financial sector collapse said to be due in part to the subprime mortgage crisis.

Blago[1] approach and simply sell the job posting of "Car Czar" to the highest bidder. The duties of the new Car Czar would not only be the review and approval of all Big Three workout plans, the Car Czar would be the one to lend them the money as well – on favorable terms and with a little governmental guarantee no doubt.

Rahmbo[2] had already leaked the list of acceptable Car Czar candidates for Congressional interviewing and interrogation. The problem was that every prominent and potential auto industry savior on the list had placed its financial future in the hands of Bernie[3] and it looked like Bernie was going to jail.

But all was not lost.

---

[1] **BLAGO**: Milorad "Rod" R. Blagojevich. He was a record holder as the first Illinois governor to ever be impeached on January 29, 2009. He made sure to jet back to his Chicago home before the Senate's final vote could formalize his civilian status and deprive him of the ride home from Springfield on the state plane. Blago notoriously tried to sell The Big BOPR's (aka Barack Obama) vacated senate seat to the highest bidder and had the misfortune of being wiretapped along the way. While he insisted he was the victim of a rush to judgment, it kinda looks like he did a Nixon and just got caught doing what everyone else has always done. It's all gonna be bleepin' golden in jail.

[2] **RAHMBO**: Rahm Emanuel, former White House Chief of Staff for The Big BOPR (aka Barack Obama); and prior to that he was a Member of the U.S. House of Representatives for Illinois' 5th Congressional District. He survived the D.C. lion's den and left the lair on September 30, 2010 to pursue his dream of being at the clandestine beck and call of The Big BOPR, or maybe even Chicago's new mayor for life.

[3] **BERNIE**: Bernard L. Madoff, Chairman and Founder of Bernard L. Madoff Investment Securities LLC, 1960. Arrested on December 11, 2008 and sentenced to 150 years of quiet meditation, Bernie currently (as of 2009) awaits his formal induction into the Ponzi Hall of Fame. AKA: the Jewish Treasury Bill and the new face of Greed. He was formerly a philanthropist, a regular family man about town, and a prominent leader in the financial services industry who gave everyone he was screwing the big KISS (keep it simple, stupid) of financial, and sometimes literal, death.

Racing straight from the Indy500 to D.C., came the shocking Car Czar wild card winner, Danica Patrick. Her well-oiled team swooped in like a pit crew wearing lip stick. She was a young, marketing machine who knew what made cars go. The time she spent under the sponsorship of subprime mortgage giant Argent/Ameriquest taught her a thing or two about loans, and her current GoDaddy sponsorship could equitably fund a portion of the Big Three bailout bridge loan in question. It was also believed that GoDaddy would give her the worldwide internet exposure she needed to raise plenty of additional capital in record time.

We overheard someone say that the new Car Czar tends to invest in what she loves, and we wondered if that, combined with a progressive, open-minded approach to doing 21st century business, would be enough to turn the Auto-Titanic around. But the real question is, who's spinning the discs in the Court of Congress now?

9

Why Bernie Made Off With 2008
December 28, 2008

There are few words to accurately describe the vibrant hum of Manhattan during the holiday season and this year was no exception, global economic collapse and all.

Standing on the corner of 53rd at 3rd in front of the Lipstick Building in Midtown, we caught sight of an announcement posted on the large lobby doors that read, "Bernie Made Off like a Pirate. Premium Office Space For Plunder." As the 17th floor sadly sat in darkness, we realized that there wasn't enough in Bernie's bank account to even pay the electric bill.

We stood there as it snowed and pondered the riches to rags story Bernie[1] had been weaving over the last several decades. Known as a man of international distinction with direct access to the highest of affluent societies, Bernie managed to build a no-questions-asked house of cards out of the world's Kings and Queens of Diamonds.

The crème de la crème must find it incomprehensible that this old man of solid reputation – and one of their own – could simultaneously outwit all regulating authorities for more years than anyone can count, and single-handedly shatter their illusion

---

[1] **BERNIE:** Bernard L. Madoff, Chairman and Founder of Bernard L. Madoff Investment Securities LLC, 1960. Arrested on December 11, 2008 and sentenced to 150 years of quiet meditation, Bernie currently (as of 2009) awaits his formal induction into the Ponzi Hall of Fame. AKA: the Jewish Treasury Bill and the new face of Greed. He was formerly a philanthropist, a regular family man about town, and a prominent leader in the financial services industry who gave everyone he was screwing the big KISS (keep it simple, stupid) of financial, and sometimes literal, death.

of being insulated and protected from society's fiscal underbelly with the prospect of imminent financial collapse and having to do without.

It's hard not to admire how Bernie cleverly cultivated an illusion of elitism by straining any prospective investor through a narrow and somewhat arbitrary snob filter. Naturally, he made it a point to reject a few every now and then. Aristocracy, nobility, gentry, bourgeoisie, nouveau riche – it really didn't matter. They all wanted in, and big bucks from a cherry-picked elite was just as good as big bucks from his own family. In spite of the occasional investor rejects, however, he was pretty much an equal opportunity shyster.

A glance **in the rear view mirror** gave us a panoramic view of the Berlin Wall as it was being dismantled in 1989; when what had once been divided and segregated, subsequently became transparent and integrated. Bernie comparably dissembled the Madoff Wall upon making confession, and the Madoff Wall had long served to separate the money secrets of the upper class from everyone else. The irony in forbidding ordinary folk membership in his private investment club was that he'd inadvertently done them a favor.

While Bernie may claim to never have heard the idiom, "Robbing Peter to pay Paul," we're certain he knows what it feels like to be caught with his hand in Peter's now empty piggy bank. Suffice it to say, he robbed some of the old Robber Barons as well.

Now that the house of cards has been blown away in a Category 5 hurricane named Bernie, no one can be sure if any grand plan or exit strategy ever truly existed. Self-preservation might've been a marginally understandable motivation for his actions, a personal quest to save face (his own, of course), until the worldwide financial realm imploded that is. Ultimately though, what Bernie did was simply travel down Bill Clinton's highway – he did it because he could.

The rich trails of Bernie's purloined funds go far and run deep. He's unquestionably left a smoldering trail of scorched earth across the world's affluent upper crust. As the charred remains of the 17th floor are sifted through, will we ever really know who Bernie burned?

10

What Comes In 3's?
January 13, 2009

We've plunged head first into a new year, and along with its fresh beginning, comes the need for a new car. The damage our jalopy sustained in the crash of 2008 was beyond repair, and we're forced to leave the junk yard masterpiece behind the Bush as we seek out a suitable replacement.

They say things always come in threes. Big 3 Automakers, Big 3 Banks, Big 3 Credit Bureaus. One could even argue "3" to be the anti-trust magic number. And now we find ourselves having to deal with all three of the Big 3's in our hot pursuit of new wheels.

As any typical car shopping American consumer knows, obtaining bank financing at preferred interest rates would be an essential first step. And being typical American consumers, we followed the necessary protocol and applied for our big purchase financing with a Big 3 Bank. What we weren't prepared for was the rejection that promptly followed.

It didn't take long to discover our credit denial was based upon an unpaid collection account erroneously listed on our Big 3 credit report. Further research indicated the collection account allegedly belonged to car fanatic Jay Leno and even he swore it wasn't his.

We knew writing letters to the Big 3 Credit Bureaus wouldn't resolve our dilemma of becoming mobile any time soon, urgency aside. Before we could even consider our next step, the phone began to ring incessantly with calls from high risk finance companies eager to provide us the loan we needed at usurious interest rates. If being debilitated with an unjust credit denial wasn't enough, the Big 3 Credit Bureaus didn't hesitate to add insult to our injury by selling our personal and confidential information to the highest bidders in the form of trigger leads.

Most of the world understands that businesses are in business to make money and the Big 3 Credit Bureaus never pretended to be non-profits; however, they are the nation's repositories of private, personal and highly confidential information and with this comes an assumed moral and fiduciary obligation to the vulnerable public whose information they routinely collect and maintain on file like the CIA. Yet, their regulated governance is dubious at best, and like the deregulated and now collapsed financial systems that chose greed over self-regulation or even (>gasp<) the greater good, they appear to have no intention of reigning themselves in.

They've caught the virus that hospitalized Wall Street.

It's easy to win the game when you make all the rules, and to hold undisputed power over the general public's financial future one person at a time can be extremely intoxicating. When the rules conveniently change like shifting sand, the public is deliberately kept intimidated by the system's illusionary complexities. Just as health insurance companies notoriously and oftentimes determine whether an individual lives or dies, the Big 3 Credit Bureaus hold the power to determine whether one financially thrives or financially dies in our credit-based economy.

A look **in the rear view mirror** swept us back to when the philosophy "Cash is King" was the rule of thumb embraced throughout nearly three-quarters of the 20th century. Three decades of Big 3 social reconditioning has made this old world practice of little benefit in today's credit driven world and basically a foreign language to Gens Y and Z.

The Madams of the Big 3 Credit Brothels appear to have amazingly formed a red-light Credit Cartel, and like all good bordellos, top priority is naturally given to the biggest paying regular customers. We're certain that isn't us and can only surmise who's paying the most for the biggest tricks.

As bottom line proliferation continues to supersede fiduciary accountability, how concerned should we be over the dissemination of our confidential information for a fee?

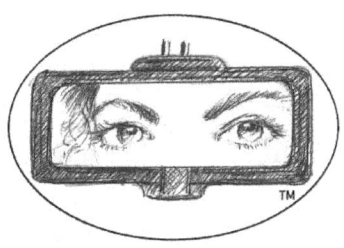

ITRVM "W" Dream Sequences

DREAM SEQUENCE:
An ITRVM Allegory where we weave things together that don't seem to go together to create a vision of things to come. We liken these to random, off-road detours along the lookout ledge of our own private Idaho. We also like to call these "Crazy Ivans."

11

Wall Street Scrooges Live The Dream
Dream Sequence, September 28, 2008

We had a dream ... and in that dream we saw the ghosts of Dot.Com's executives from Christmas past visiting the Wall Street Executive Scrooges of today. The ghosts of Dot.Com showed the Ebenezers of Wall Street that it really wasn't so bad living on 8 weeks of unemployment, peanut butter & jelly sandwiches, and having only $9.28 in their wallets to hold them over for the next 5 days until their unemployment check arrives.

As the Scrooges were shown their future, they could see that it soon wouldn't matter they were made to join the ranks of all the other discards from a collapsed high rolling past because not only would they have the fanciest (and latest) computer models with all the ergonomic accoutrements, they'd also have high speed internet and the Monster Job Board.

And then we woke up and realized this was no dream, it was a nightmare, but whose nightmare?

12

Who's Burning Bush?
Dream Sequence, October 16, 2008

We had a dream … and in that dream we saw the last 8 years epitomized in a mirage of President George W. Bush wandering the desert wilderness with the masses of a nation in tow. He was holding the staff of a commander-in-chief in his right hand like a beacon, yet navigating like a blind man without the benefit of any higher guidance. Our dream showed him eventually finding his way to Mount Vernon (home to the original George "W") and his subsequent discovery of that big burning rosebush in the middle of the Rose Garden.

The fiery rosebush began to speak. "W" clearly anticipated the deliverance of a divine message as if he were Moses but instead got the booming voice of Richard Milhous Nixon who simply said, "Don't even bother looking behind this burning bush; there's nothing here." Nixon continued on in a mumble, "And they thought I was bad …"

And then we woke up and marveled at history's propensity for repetition. It made us wonder whether we still had 32 more years of wandering in the desert wilderness left to go.

So does this also mean that "W" will be denied favorable entry into the promised land of our history books upon his exodus?

13

Will The Lame Duck Be Flying South For The Winter?
Dream Sequence, November 1, 2008

We had a dream ... and in that dream we saw Florida putting its post-presidential election ballot counters to good use as former President George W. Bush wins a decisive victory in his run for Mayor of Guantanamo Bay.

Too much vacation time went against his workaholic nature and how to spend his twilight years after retirement from the White House in a way that continued to touch the lives of the people was of paramount importance. More important still was his bottom line, yet staring him in the face was an inconvenient truth. He was no math whiz, but he knew without a doubt that his social security checks just weren't going to be enough to maintain the lifestyle he'd grown quite fond of.

Our dream made it painfully obvious that XP "W"[1] didn't spend the last 8 years in D.C. and not learn a thing. He recognized a winning team when it was assembled on his behalf, so he promptly set out to place several of his favorites in key positions in an attempt to re-create some of that "Emperor's New Clothes" type of magic he'd grown accustomed to.

---

[1] **XP "W"**: Ex-President George W. Bush, 43rd President of the United States of America, Inc., officially sworn in to office January 20, 2001. He served two disastrous 4-year terms then finally crashed and burned his way out on January 19, 2009. He was succeeded by The Big BOPR (aka Barack Obama).

Mayor George firmly believed he'd gotten things off to a good start when Rush Limbaugh[1] accepted the position of Hostel Camp Manager and Activities Director. In determining the next appointee, even he knew it was critical that Guantanamo Bay's new Mayor have a big thug (someone who was silent but carried a big shotgun) to put out in front. And without question, Sheriff Dick had an unbeatable track record. In his mind, though, the icing on the cake was when his new BFF, Paris Hilton, agreed to join the team as Director of Marketing and Promotion.

Paris didn't waste one fabulous minute in putting together a highly impressive VIP guest list for the new Mayor's inaugural celebration. She managed to procure RSVPs from some surprising world dignitaries, like Hugo Chavez (Venezuela), Vladimir Putin (Russia), Bashar al-Assad (Syria), and Mahmoud Ahmadinejad (Iran), to name a few.

In his new position as Hostel Camp MAD-man, Rush's first big maneuver was to re-open Camp X-Ray under its new name, Camp S+M. Paris immediately began a high profile across-the-globe marketing blitz spotlighting the camp's new honeymoon-on-the-racks package for only the most discriminating of couples looking to stretch their limits. And Paris wisely included in her saucy promos something to attract the seasoned couple who believed marriage was torture by offering them the perfect setting to take their torment to another level.

No detail was too small and MAD-man Rush always made sure to have plenty of painkillers of the potent prescription variety on

---

[1] **RUSH LIMBAUGH**: Limbaugh was an opinionated, loud and outspoken American conservative political commentator who hosted "The Rush Limbaugh Show" radio show from 1988 until his death in 2021. He was arrested for prescription drug fraud in 2006 due, in part, to his addiction to painkillers; OxyContin being a particular favorite.

hand for distribution to his special guests as they required. He reckoned too it would encourage them to stay longer.

And then we woke up, and got a **side mirror** glimpse of Castro, in his final hours, making one last executive decision to finally deposit all of those Guantanamo Bay rent checks we've been sending him since 1959, then of course, he raised the rent.

In pondering George's short attention span and dubious intellect, are we safe in assuming this will be enough to keep him contained?

14

Washingstone B.C.
Dream Sequence, November 14, 2008

We had a dream ... and in that dream we saw our favorite modern Stone Age families strike it rich with a newfound energy source called crude oil, and make that big move out of the Bedrock burbs into the political tar pits of Washingstone B.C., where any Neanderthal can have an effect on the evolution of the species homo sapien.

In our dream, it was easy to see how one lifestyle change typically leads to another and having wealth did afford certain options one might not otherwise have. So with the revenues that flowed in like the oil, we saw Wilma and Betty opt to stay behind to raise Pebbles and Bamm-Bamm and do their thing in Bedrock, as Barney and Fred made the decision to move out together and finally get that place of their very own in a nice Bostone community.

It didn't take Barney F. Rubble[1] (D-MA) long to reach the political heights vital to fulfilling his altruistic dream of positively influencing public policy for the benefit of every primate under his jurisdiction. Repetitive evolutionary cycles were nothing new in the long history of an upstanding man, and we watched in our dream as Barney worked diligently to promote legislative measures he felt were necessary to curb the collective homo

---

[1] **BARNEY FRANK**: Frank was a prominent gay Democratic politician who represented the state of Massachusetts in the House of Representatives from 1981 to 2013. He also served as Chairman of the House Financial Services Committee during "The Great Recession" from 2007 to 2011 and was a leading co-sponsor of the 2010 Dodd-Frank Act which basically overhauled financial regulation for almost every part of the nation's financial services industry.

sapien's tendency toward devolutionary back-stepping, which oftentimes occurred when too much power was held in the hands of too few and when deregulated greediness prevailed.

Suffice it to say, Barney was appalled when Mr. Slate – CEO of the nation's largest Stone Quarry which now looked more like a Strip Mine – held out his hand looking for a large chunk of the newly legislated Big Boulder Bailout[1] ("BBB"). The quarry had been cutting costs all right and Mr. Slate could prove it. His big-wigged henchmen had just laid off 75% of the quarry workers and Fred was one of them.

Unfortunately, even the cost savings that strategy realized wasn't enough to cover the enormous, yet still unpaid, contractual obligations now pressing him for immediate satisfaction. Not only was his own bonus past due, so were those of his crony bigwigs. It was critical to the Stone Quarry's continued economic survival that he keep his mis-management team in place and $40 Billion clams was just what he needed to do it. This was, Mr. Slate insisted, in the long term best interest of Neanderthals everywhere.

The Stone Quarry wasn't the only pit deep in the hole. The Stone Age car makers were way behind the times. They'd persisted in manufacturing energy inefficient cars that did little but produce foot calluses and wondered why no one was buying. Surprisingly, it never crossed their minds that maybe Mr. Slate of

---

[1] **TARP** (Troubled Asset Relief Program) is a direct result of the Emergency Economic Stabilization Act of October, 2008 (aka "Bank Bailout of 2008" and "Wall Street Bailout") enacted by President George W. Bush which allowed the U.S. government to use taxpayer funds to the tune of $700 Billion to purchase toxic assets and equity from failing banks/financial institutions in order to prop up and prevent a total financial sector collapse said to be due in part to the subprime mortgage crisis.

the Stone-Quarry-now-Strip-Mine was partially responsible for their slow car sales.

All they saw was that Mr. Slate and his bigwigs got a big piece of the BBB without having to give up much more than lay a few workers off, and they wanted some of that action too. With a friend like Speaker of the Cave, Nancy Pebblosi, pleading their case in exchange for a new pearl necklace, they were very hopeful.

Of the three car makers, the loudest and most demanding was "Great Mastodon" (also known as "GM"). "Carnivore" felt that if Lee Iarocka could do it, so could Nancy Pebblosi. They were in. And not to be left behind, "Brontosaurus", maker of the ever popular Bronto, was certainly expecting its lion's share of the dole as well.

And then we woke up, and remembered that no matter how dire the straits, The Great Gazoo never seemed to appear when he was called. Will The Great Gazoo ever show up?

15

World Forwards Final Bill To "W" In Crawford, TX
Dream Sequence, November 30, 2008

We had a dream ... and in that dream we saw a panic that far surpassed the hysteria witnessed 8 years ago as 1999 was drawing to a close. The fear of '99 simmered and swelled on the certain knowledge that our world as we knew it would fatefully end when Y2K made its inevitable entree at midnight on December 31.

Y2K's frightful millennium shift ultimately proved to be unfounded, or so it seemed on January 1, 2000 anyway. Nevertheless it didn't take us long to realize that we really did have every reason to be afraid, for later in the new millennium's first year, George W. Bush was elected to his first 4-year term as President. From that moment on, we watched the world we'd once known begin to steadily deteriorate, until the fatal economic barrage hit mid-2008.

In our dream we could see that as the end of 2008 fast approached, a powerful fear gripped the world once again. But instead of hiding out in bomb shelters with stored food stuffs waiting for the end of time, the masses collectively responded in revolutionary anger as they joined forces and decided to finally take matters into their own hard working hands.

The internet spread word of the People's revolt like wildfire: December 31, 2008 had been declared International BK Day - BK8 for short. It was predicted that every court in the world would be packed to overflowing as the unruly multitudes simultaneously filed their legal version of Chapter 7 Bankruptcy. The People were done carrying the financial burden of international hedge fund greed and corporate mismanagement on their backs.

And then we woke up, and realized that it was probably no coincidence the People's BK8 insurgency came at the disastrous conclusion of "W's" second term as President. So if capitalism is bankrupt and the People are bankrupt, who will be expected to pick up the tab and fund the now bankrupt system?

16

Who's Talking Like A Pirate Now?
Dream Sequence, December 7, 2008

We had a dream ... and in that dream we heard the Pirates of Somalia[1] crooning the Robber Baron song of old about how exploitation was justified under the guise of bringing order to the industrial chaos of the day.

It's one thing to throw caution to the wind while plundering the Indian Ocean for ransom money when there's nothing to lose and everything to gain. But 2008 had been an extremely profitable year. Undeniably, it was time to legitimize their booty and foster a long term economic enrichment plan which included putting solid growth strategies in to place. And like the historic Robber Barons of a century ago, this practical approach would ultimately obscure the source of their loot and afford them the opportunity to later gloss it over in some high profile form of philanthropy.

In our dream we watched the Somalian Pirates implement the first stage of their plan to go legit by orchestrating a sit down with Erik Prince of Blackwater[2] Worldwide on friendly ground in Dubai – the Pirates planned to incorporate and take legal ownership of a sanctioned international port of their own. Everyone knew that Blackwater's mercenaries were quickly

---

[1] **SOMALIAN PIRATES**: The Somali Pirates and their highly lucrative ransom demands were a major threat to international shipping and boating off the Somalian peninsula/Horn of Africa during the war in Somalia from 2006 to 2009. Somalia was considered a failed state until 2012.

[2] **BLACKWATER**: Blackwater Worldwide was an American military contractor (mercenary army) founded by Erik Prince who was a Navy SEAL and CIA asset. It was reputed to be VP Dick Cheney's mercenary army of choice during the Bush Administration from 2001 to 2008. Blackwater changed its name to Xe in 2009.

running out of good paying work and Somalia's Pirates desperately needed Blackwater's help in navigating these new directional waters. It was clearly a win-win all the way around, and magic happened that day in Dubai.

Nothing can grease the wheels of speed like loads of cash. The Horn of Africa had its terrain forever altered when Blackwater rapidly established a new state-of-the-art training facility in Somalia's lawless Puntland region, now re-named BLACKHORN. Blackhorn was located just east of the former pirate hideaway Port of Eyl, which had now been sanctioned as their internationally recognized shipping port officially re-named PORT OF BLACK EYE. No mercenary adventure of this magnitude could ever be complete without the perfect mission statement and Blackhorn's call was now "Robbin' the Hood."

Our dream then turned toward the plan's second stage: to form a pirate bank of their own. If the Red Shield[1] could finance the exploitive goals of Carnegie and Rockefeller over a century ago, then the newly chartered SIMOLEON BANK could legitimately finance their enterprise and launder the shillings as well. After opening its flagship bank in Port of Black Eye, long term business plan projections provided for additional Simoleon Bank branch openings in strategic locations to include Mogadishu, Dubai, Liberia, and of course, Tehran.

What we found ironic in all of this was that in their attempts to protect their own interests by going legit, the Pirates of Somalia unwittingly invigorated their country's economy and created a stability in government, albeit Blackhorn militia, the likes of which had never been experienced by a majority of Somalia's current population.

---

[1] **RED SHIELD**: The Rothschild Banking Family.

And then we woke up and could see how the world yields a certain commiserative tolerance for those who act with moral compromise while on the quest for great wealth. Is it possible to walk the path of great riches and have room for genuine altruism to walk concurrently beside it, or must one path be pursued solely to the exclusion of the other?

17

Was That Wingtip A Size 10?
Dream Sequence, December 21, 2008

We had a dream ... and in that dream we saw a pensive George W. Bush receiving his final invite from French Prezy Nicolas Sarkozy for an Adieu Party at the exquisite Chateau de Versailles on January 21, 2009 – the anniversary of French King Louis XVI's beheading.

Our dream made it obvious that "W's" guest list just wasn't as world-class as it used to be which seemed to take the pressure off. There were few to impress at this party so he could comfortably let it all hang out and be detente-free. Opened Budweiser can in hand, he took leave of the merrymakers in favor of a solitary stroll through the Chateau.

It wasn't long before XP "W"[1] found himself standing smack dab in the middle of Versailles' Hall of Mirrors. The last 8 years had been somewhat stressful, and while he stared upon his full reflection in one of the 17 large mirrors lining the Hall, he couldn't help but admire how well he'd aged like a fine wine through it all.

Before he could even stumble on to his next thought, George's eyes glazed over like he'd been hypnotized and what came next can only be likened to an Alice-in-the-looking-glass adventure, except that he'd been sucked into a time warp that plopped him down into the sunset of the French Revolution 216 years earlier,

---

[1] **XP "W"**: Ex-President George W. Bush, 43rd President of the United States of America, Inc., officially sworn in to office January 20, 2001. He served two disastrous 4-year terms then finally crashed and burned his way out on January 19, 2009. He was succeeded by The Big BOPR (aka Barack Obama).

on January 21, 1793. Inconceivably, George recognized himself in a previous incarnation as King Louis XVI of France at the time of his execution.

George watched himself in the body of Louis resolutely mount the guillotine scaffold with as much dignity as he could muster and attempt to make a small speech reasserting his innocence. His speech was rudely interrupted by a shout exploding from deep within the witnessing crowd of the revolutionary cry, "Liberte', egalite', fraternite'!!" And then a large shoe came flying through the air toward his head. George as Louis was agile enough even then to dodge that first fast moving trajectory, but not agile enough to parry the countless other shoes and boots that quickly followed.

Those speedy projectiles almost saved the executioner from doing his job, but not really. George subsequently saw his Louis-head roll into the dirt after the guillotine's blade swiftly fell, and watched as the mob dipped their stockings in his blood as it dripped to the ground.

Snapping out of it, George suddenly had a headache and wanted to leave his own party. As he approached the waiting stretch limo, the Adieu Party guests rallied around the courtyard to see him off. No sooner had his limo begun its forward roll when the shoes of every guest present went flying high into the air, followed by raucous whoops and cheers in celebration. C'est la vie!

And then we woke up and could see why Louis XVI's miserable failure as Monarch of France ultimately resulted in his assignation with the guillotine on the heels of the French Revolution. Yet somehow, King Louis had managed to inadvertently make a profound contribution to the victory of America's War of

Independence from King George of England and all of his madness. We wondered if "W" consciously intended to destroy today as President what he'd helped build centuries earlier as King.

It seems very few of us get a do-over of this magnitude. Is it possible "W" will get an incarnated third time in the Rulership ring, say around 2200?

18

What Happened To My Other Half?
Dream Sequence, January 6, 2009

We had a dream ... and in that dream we encountered quantum physics at its purest when the hidden veil separating our dimension from all others dropped and granted us entry into some parallel universe where anything can happen.

It wasn't initially clear why our interdimensional journey began at the George Town Hospital on Grand Cayman Island until we came to the maternity ward and beheld Barbara Bush breathing like a metronome in true Lamaze fashion as she suffered through heavy contractions. In the bed next to her was an Iranian woman named Sayeed laboring toward a similar delivery of her own.

Under the night's luminous full moon, both women were wheeled side-by-side into the delivery room where they concurrently gave birth to sons. Barbara had twin boys of the not so identical variety and Sayeed delivered a son who sadly didn't survive beyond his third tiny gasp. The overall chaotic frenzy of the maternity ward that night, combined with the fact that both women had lost consciousness during childbirth due to gas mask sedation, paved the way for a baby mix-up having unforeseen consequences.

Barbara was disoriented upon waking and kept insisting she was in Georgetown, Massachusetts. She had absolutely no memory of giving birth to very dissimilar looking twins – one light skinned of average size and one dark skinned imp. And when Sayeed awoke in a comparable mind fog, the nurse quickly pushed Barbara's dark skinned twin into her arms. Sayeed left the hospital for return to Iran with her new baby Mahmoud at the same time Barbara departed for the States with her fair baby George.

As our dream continued its weave through the growth and developmental dynamics of these twins separated at birth, it was obvious that the scientific limits of nature vs. nurture would be fully tested. Observations noted were:

NURTURE:
Both boys encountered a lifetime of maternal negligent. Barbara never fully bonded with George because she always felt something was missing, and Sayeed never bonded with Mahmoud because he just didn't look right.

George was raised with a silver spoon in his mouth. He was insulated, sheltered and rarely had to work hard for anything. He attended all of the right schools, yet had a proclivity for partying and schmoozing, nor did he care if his performance was marginal as long as everyone was happy.

Mahmoud, on the other hand, was raised as a poor peasant and was lucky to have a spoon at all. He was focused, driven and intelligent; an engineer and self-made man who worked hard to achieve greatness.

Revolution catapulted Mahmoud into power, while power for George was purchased.

NATURE:
Recessive genes and junk DNA sequences played themselves out all over this passion play. When the fertilized egg did what it did in utero, it was unquestionable that Mahmoud got the bigger brain genes and George got the leftovers. Conversely, it was

George who got the bigger physique genes and Mahmoud got the leftovers.

Physical discrepancies aside, the twins were remarkably similar and they reflected mirror images in behavior, perceptions, limitations, and charisma.

George and Mahmoud both possessed bi-polar personalities – an inferiority complex one day and "it's my way or the highway" the next. Driven by a need to rule, both identically demonstrated their power with bull-headed stubbornness and a refusal to see any unacceptable reality because everything was going to be fine.

Religious piety was a mutual priority as well. They each believed their chosen theological road to salvation was the only road resulting in a divisive intolerance for the differing belief systems of others. These personal theological preferences typically took precedence over logic or the collective greater good.

The ultimate irony, though, was their shared and acute loathing for each other. It was as if they unconsciously recognized the common DNA strands that bound them together, and resented the fact that while apart, they were individually only one half of the whole.

And then we woke up with an overwhelming sense of déjà vu' and wondered if the outcome might've been significantly altered had those twin boys been switched in the reverse at birth. Is it possible the state of the world would look different today had Mahmoud Ahmadinejad been President of the United States and George W. Bush the President of Iran?

19

So Long, Farewell, Auf Wiedersehen, Good Night
January 19, 2009

With our own sound of music, we finally sing our "adieu grande" to the old regime. Along with its passing – and we're even a little sad to say this – goes our "**W**" Headliner Series in which every story and dream sequence headline ceremoniously began in the letter "**W**."

So long, farewell, auf wiedersehen, good night …

Goodbye, Goodbye, Goodbye!

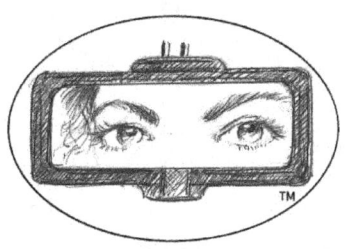

ITRVM Blog Series

20

Taking The Bull By The Horns
January 26, 2009

As the world forlornly entered the "Year of the Bull," the United States inaugurated a new Bull-Ox President in The Big BOPR[1], and it seems the masses have conceded that a new plan for steering the old ox cart is destined to enter in with it.

The global balance sheets of today are diametrically opposed to those of the inflated bully days. Devastation abounds and few escaped. Even the big Bull that had been driving Merrill Lynch got yoked before it finally got lynched.

To look **in the rear view mirror** is to see how Wall Street eminence and psychopathology are surprisingly interrelated. Any stellar personality profile for the successful Wall Street tycoon apparently must include core character traits consistent with those of a true psychopath – unbridled narcissism, strong sense of entitlement, firm sense of impunity, and lack of remorse, to name a few.

When comparing some commonly observed character traits of Wall Street's two most recent celebrity headliners, I-ROB[2] and Bernie[3], we noticed some interesting parallels:

---

[1] **THE BIG BOPR:** Barack Obama, President and "Renegade" (his Secret Service code name). He was the successor to President George W. Bush (aka XP "W") after being "sworn" in to office on January 20, 2009 as the 44th President of the United States of America, Inc. AKA Traitor 44.

[2] **I-ROB**: John A. Thain, former CEO of Merrill Lynch who resigned on January 22, 2009, right before Bank of America CEO Ken Lewis could sack him. Mr. Fix-It proposed the shotgun wedding between Merrill and BofA and their CEOs, which abruptly ended in annulment barely 3 months later (didn't something like that happen with Rene' Zellweger and Kenny Chesney?). BofA gobbled up Merrill's enormous deficit and naturally passed the tab on to the taxpayers in the

I-ROB
Personality: Cold, icy, emotionally detached, lacking in people skills, some level of charisma.

Office Décor: Warm and cozy. He paid $1.22 Million to make his office feel more like home.

BERNIE
Personality: Affable, congenial, charismatic, some level of aloofness.

Office Décor: Cold, icy, stark, color schemes limited to black, white, and shades of gray. This theme was prevalent throughout his offices in NYC, London and even his private jet.

True to psychopathic form, both of these big boys have systematically implemented comprehensive impression management regimens resulting in carefully cultivated public personas, yet at the same time they're unable to control their varying levels of OCD and control freak attributes.

Our unofficial clinical assessment has classified them overall as a hybrid fusion of LAB-Rat[1] and Moldy Old White Bread[2].

---

form of TARP bailout funding. I-ROB smoothly managed to expend $1.22 Million to make his office feel more like home, and to secretly disburse $4 Billion in early employee bonuses before dashing off to Vail, Colorado for a year-end ski holiday just as Merrill's $15.3 Billion 2008 4Q loss was announced. AKA "I-ROBOT" for his mechanical coldness, void of emotion and intense financial focus.

[3] **BERNIE**: Bernard L. Madoff, Chairman and Founder of Bernard L. Madoff Investment Securities LLC, 1960. Arrested on December 11, 2008 and sentenced to 150 years of quiet meditation, Bernie currently (as of 2009) awaits his formal induction into the Ponzi Hall of Fame. AKA: the Jewish Treasury Bill and the new face of Greed. He was formerly a philanthropist, a regular family man about town, and a prominent leader in the financial services industry who gave everyone he was screwing the big KISS (keep it simple, stupid) of financial, and sometimes literal, death.

We got word that XP "W"[1] didn't hesitate to forward his moving van up to I-ROB once he was settled back on the Texas ranch. If they could get him out of the White House in 5 hours flat, they could certainly get I-ROB out of his newly renovated, homey little Merrill Lynch office posthaste. It sure felt good to give back to one of his loyal supporters. Unfortunately, a Special Air Mission 28000 free helicopter ride was off limits and not offered with the get-out-of-town-fast benefits package.

The autopsy of 2008 will likely be underway for many decades to come, and undoubtedly traditional business standards and mores

---

[1] **LAB-RAT** (Archetype): These are the fringe skulkers who hover just below the radar – like they're there but not really part of anything. They appear to be pleasant and normal and give the illusion of making some sort of contribution, yet underneath they're really cold fish with no true need for emotional substance or interpersonal depth. LAB-Rats navigate within a highly compartmentalized world that revolves solely around them which manifests itself in the form of brain-body incongruencies. It's almost as if some unseen master has strategically placed remote-controlled electronic stimulus patches all over their body and knows just when to trigger the switch. This brain-body disconnect gives them little instinct for even the most rudimentary consideration for the needs of another, resulting in a narcissistic drive to achieve their goals at any cost, without conscience or accountability. Busy scurrying and always on the go, and clearly no time for quiet introspection sans distraction, LAB-Rats can frequently be found flying the redeye from L.A. to Boston and back again with Blackberry in hand and a GPS perpetually connected to the unseen master. Evasive and duplicitous by nature, they might even tell you they live in France.

[2] **MOLDY OLD WHITE BREAD, or "MOWB"** (Archetype): A tasty depiction of a human anachronism who routinely derives sustenance from stale, inedible, and moldy ways of thinking, while advocating modus operandi that is firmly entrenched in standards set by the "Old Guard." MOWBs are not conservatively categorized or necessarily stereotyped by gender, age, race, culture, or even political party affiliation; but usually reveal their unmistakable MOWB-ness with a mindset deeply rooted in entitlement, arrogance, superiority and double standards.

[1] **XP "W"**: Ex-President George W. Bush, 43rd President of the United States of America, Inc., officially sworn in to office January 20, 2001. He served two disastrous 4-year terms then finally crashed and burned his way out on January 19, 2009. He was succeeded by The Big BOPR (aka Barack Obama).

will be deeply probed and questioned under the coming post-mortem examination.

As for I-ROB, we won't hold our breath waiting for his mea culpa. As for his comfy $1.22 Million office, it looks like he learned the hard way that you never, ever have an office better than your new boss. But what we really want to know is who gets his $1,405 waste basket?

21

Catching A Few Xe's
February 15, 2009

It wasn't until the final hours of Era XP "W"[1] that we really began to notice the unquestionable symptoms of Bush Flu[2] in those who'd once been considered immune.

We bled dollars as the legislative powers intravenously administered the large cash infusions these untouchables demanded to staunch further dehydration of their formerly fluid bank accounts. And just because we paid for the medical attention they'd felt entitled to receive apparently didn't mean they believed us mutually entitled to an accounting of how our blood money was spent.

With the recent changing of the Old Guard comes the abrupt realization that economic survival is now demanding that everyone change with it as well, and one look **in the rear view mirror** at the many faces of Madonna can show us the way. A master of cyclical reinvention and repackaging, Madonna has successfully managed to keep that "Queen of Pop" crown firmly placed upon her head with no end in sight to her reign.

---

[1] **XP "W"**: Ex-President George W. Bush, 43rd President of the United States of America, Inc., officially sworn in to office January 20, 2001. He served two disastrous 4-year terms then finally crashed and burned his way out on January 19, 2009. He was succeeded by The Big BOPR (aka Barack Obama).

[2] **BUSH FLU**: A highly resistant and uncooperative viral strain that was released from the golden parachutes strapped to the backs of financial district CEOs as they were ejected by their Board of Directors and pushed out of Air Force One. Subsequent studies eventually confirmed that the virus was carried and transmitted through the small air-borne drops of crude oil that leeched from the edges of the golden parachutes upon deployment. Symptoms include: Great Depression. No money in the bank. Your bank's ATM machine holds your debit card hostage and instead spits out a government I.O.U. by way of a receipt in the form of Federal Reserve Notes.

It comes as no surprise then that ex-VP Dick Cheney's Iraqi goon squad formerly known as Blackwater[1] has officially changed its name to "Xe" (pronounced "Z", oh duh). Word on the street is that Erik Prince had consulted with rock 'n roll Hall of Famer and artist formerly known as Prince before coming up with the new name.

Like many of the old courtiers who so smoothly distanced themselves from the debris of a bygone regime, Blackwater-now-Xe recognized its economic survival demanded they quickly follow Madonna's lead. Of course, the bear paw logo synonymous with what used to be called Blackwater would go the way of the old name and be immediately replaced with a flaming rapier's 3-stroke swish reminiscent of Zorro's "Z."

Xe didn't waste one precious "new name" moment before announcing itself the global one-stop shopping source for world class services in the fields of security, stability, aviation, training and logistics. While they would never publicly admit to their friendly affiliation with ex-VP Cheney, they've secretly agreed to give him complimentary target practice since he'll only have secret service protection until 2019.

Along with the departure of the cash flow once provided by the old regime went Blackwater's former image and old loyalties.

Most of us know that mercenary loyalties will always follow the gold, regardless of where their training facilities are located. So who will be the highest bidder now?

---

[1] **BLACKWATER**: Blackwater Worldwide was an American military contractor (mercenary army) founded by Erik Prince who was a Navy SEAL and CIA asset. It was reputed to be VP Dick Cheney's mercenary army of choice during the Bush Administration from 2001 to 2008. Blackwater changed its name to Xe in 2009.

22

Big Brother Goes Hard ... Drive, That Is
February 27, 2009

We knew the bill would be a whopper when The Big BOPR[1] finally did the math and prepared to pass the collection basket. The White House reckoning from above will now require every taxpayer to toss more than $12,000 into that collection basket when it's passed down the aisle.

Forwarding the final bill to XP "W"[2] in Crawford, TX was certainly a tempting dream sequence; however, we've been slapped hard with the reality that personal accountability by those in positions of power has heretofore been virtually non-existent. So instead of sending XP "W" an invoice, we've elected to send him a thank you note for plunging a final thrust straight into the heart of the Old Guard.

Seems XP "W" didn't stay on the Crawford ranch for long anyway. He and Laura decided to call Dallas home, and the media made sure everyone knew they'd purchased a humble estate in the well-heeled suburb of Preston Hollow. Understandably, George felt it important to be close to Laura's alma mater where his think tank and presidential library were to be housed.

---

[1] **THE BIG BOPR:** Barack Obama, President and "Renegade" (his Secret Service code name). He was the successor to President George W. Bush (aka XP "W") after being "sworn" in to office on January 20, 2009 as the 44th President of the United States of America, Inc. AKA Traitor 44.

[2] **XP "W":** Ex-President George W. Bush, 43rd President of the United States of America, Inc., officially sworn in to office January 20, 2001. He served two disastrous 4-year terms then finally crashed and burned his way out on January 19, 2009. He was succeeded by The Big BOPR (aka Barack Obama).

A few simple keystrokes on whitepages.com gave us instant access to (what used to be considered) highly personal information cross-linked within the public internet domain, and made finding George and Laura's new home mailing address and phone number effortless. The ease with which we successfully obtained the Bush's information was both gratifying and alarming at the same time.

There are two sides to every coin, and when the pendulum swings to the extreme in one direction, it'll always swing back to the opposite extreme before ultimately finding its balance.

The Old Guard's excessively secretive ways are being steadily replaced with the public's demand for transparency in all things, even at the expense of dignity and self-respect. The popular trend toward voyeuristic fascination, and even obsession, with the private life business of others is indisputable when considering the innumerable reality TV shows dominating network programming on a daily basis throughout the world.

A look **in the rear view mirror** showed us Steve Martin screaming, "the phone book is here!" in the movie "The Jerk." It was a reminder of when everyone's phone number was automatically listed in the large white pages telephone book and if someone wanted their phone number unlisted, it was. Full stop.

Today's Peeping-Tom movement toward complete private sector transparency (some would call that an oxymoron) basically puts every man, woman and child under 24/7 surveillance and makes it essentially impossible to preserve any modicum of personal privacy. We can't help but wonder how much we really need to know about each other's private lives and what would constitute crossing the line of just too much information in current society.

As our personal and private data flows freely across the world wide web under the guise of freedom of information, social networking websites and the techno pros within large data repositories for identity theft are systematically archiving and cultivating that flow for future use.

The paranoia expressed in previous decades revolving around the watchful eyes of Big Brother rings hollow as we now find society simply handing it all over willingly, without hesitation or limitation. Do we really have control over our identities and private lives anymore?

23

Barbie, BFF
March 14, 2009

It was our understanding that one major economic motivation for paying bailout mega-bucks to rescue the Big Banks was so they could turn around and lend that money back to us. Recent experience has shown this plan to be highly flawed, however, because the Big 3 have flatly refused to finance our replacement car, credit report dispute notwithstanding.

Luckily our old friend, Barbie, preferred driving the Jeep and generously offered us her classic pink corvette convertible to drive as long as we liked. Nostalgia ensued when she handed us the fuzzy pink key chain.

Over the last half century, we've together witnessed our "Beaver Cleaver" society morph into a "Z Generation," and although many of us oftentimes feel left behind, our friend Barbie has admirably kept pace without missing a beat.

Fresh out of Willow, Wisconsin, she burst onto the public scene in the late 1950's. She was already ahead of her time and everybody wanted what she had. To achieve the iconic status she did typically subjects one to perverse microscopic scrutiny and interminable pea-green-with-envy attacks. Barbie was no exception.

She purchased her Malibu Dream House in 1962 and led the charge for equal rights when she found her voice (with a pull string ring) in 1968. We cheered her on as she blazed trails through the 1970's as a PanAm Stewardess, an Astronaut, and even an Olympic Skier. Barbie showed us there was no limit to what we could do when she deftly mixed her many formidable careers with rock star partying, silver lame' and platform spiked heels through the heady disco days of the 1980's. The 1990's then saw her serving our country in every branch of the military, doing the rodeo circuit as Western Barbie, and traveling the country on her Biker Barbie Harley.

Regrettably, Father Time spares no one and to fully embrace life's natural cycles can be difficult at best, so it's no surprise that at 50, she secretly knows herself as Menopausal Barbie, while the media proceeds to sneeringly refer to her as Cougar Barbie. Frankly, those new tattoos she just had to get the other day did nothing to favorably replace the snarky Cougar reference with a more fashionable Inked Barbie.

The corvette's engine purred like a kitten when we turned the key but was promptly drowned out when an old cassette tape stuck in the tape deck began to regurgitate the screaming voice of Tyra Banks out of every loud speaker, "Body Image! Body Image! Body Image!" Tyra's tyrannical loop about girls growing up too fast in today's culture with unrealistic "perfect" body expectations has merit to be sure, yet it seems a little late for her to be preaching from that altar – especially since Tyra made her fortune long ago with a Victoria's Secret soft porn body image she can no longer maintain. Clearly, Father Time knows everybody's address.

Pulling away from Barbie's Dream House, we couldn't help but sadly glance **in the rear view mirror** at the large "For Sale" sign posted on her front lawn. Even with all of her work experience (for it seems her curriculum vitae never included Wall Street Banker Barbie), Barbie managed to end up with an Option ARM mortgage and was forced to sell her dream house in a down market or lose it to the bank in foreclosure.

Relocating to West Virginia was definitely out of the question. The Barbie Ban Bill was just passed and a restraining order has been placed upon her measurements. She's Outlaw Barbie now.

The end of an era is upon us.

The feminine form has historically proven to be a direct reflection of cultural priorities throughout the generations, and somehow Barbie shockingly became emblematic of what was considered perfect female form for nigh 4 generations, albeit unrealistic and unattainable.

Perhaps it's time for our old friend to embrace her age with dignity and bow out gracefully. When Barbie's image finally becomes passe', who will boldly step into her high heeled shoes?

24

The American Myth
March 31, 2009

Once upon a time there was a land of plenty and it was called America.

For more than a century, America held its brilliant torch high and boldly announced to the world, "Give me your tired, your poor, your huddled masses yearning to breathe free, the wretched refuse of your teeming shore. Send these, the homeless, tempest-tossed to me...," never believing that many of its very own could work hard and become just that: tired, poor, homeless and tempest-tossed.

On its maiden voyage to America in 1912, the RMS Titanic hit an iceberg. The grand ship's SOS distress signal swiftly surrendered herself to the sea along with 68% of her passengers. This tragedy sadly pales in comparison to today's economic Titanic which has collided head-on with the massive iceberg effects of deregulation, and is swiftly sinking – nose down and props up in stink bug position.

America's economic ship began to visibly take on water as deregulation seeped throughout the energy and utility sectors, and we got our first real glimpse of the end with the Enron fiasco in 2001. As the systematic deregulation of our financial systems surged forth, monopolies steadily squeezed out healthy competition and the notion of self-regulation proved to be oxymoronic.

Many of the economy passengers on board America's modern-day Titanic have already been tossed overboard and feel abandoned, with new ones joining them under water every day. They appear to have little choice but to desperately cling to the side of the sinking ship.

With this changing of the tide have come the waves of opportunistic bottom feeders, rising to the surface, intent to prey upon those desperately holding on in order to benefit financially from their misfortune by offering the empty promise of a life raft … for a non-refundable, no guarantees, paid-up-front-and-in-advance fee, of course.

The overwhelming eruption of various niche scams designed solely to take advantage of our current economic SOS – restructuring, modification, workout, and employment recruiting services that expect payment of substantial up-front fees and premeditatedly provide little but hollow promises – reveals an unsettling lack of social cohesiveness or sense of community, let alone any rudimentary compassion for the suffering of another.

Some might simply dismiss this as just another face, or extension, of the very greed that created the crisis to begin with.

In the rear view mirror we can plainly see how Black Tuesday on October 29, 1929 ushered in a decade long Great Depression which bred a survival psychosis of holocaustic proportions that permeated core belief systems at a cellular level for the next 3 generations.

Should history prove itself an accurate gauge, it would stand to reason that the emotional repercussions of today's Great Depression will likewise deeply influence the core belief systems of generations to come. The immediate effects of the now emerging survival psychology will undoubtedly result in the loss of an entire generation of 30 to 40-something investors who'll no longer trust the broken system, let alone choose to invest in it.

While this lost generation of investors may cautiously elect to opt out of what used to be considered the American dream, they're still indisputably left carrying the bulk of today's economic collapse and financial crisis on their backs.

What do you believe is worth investing in today?

25

Greed Goes Underground
April 13, 2009

April Fool's Day saw G20 delegates from the world's largest economies converge in London for a common problem-solving objective: how to halt today's global fiscal freefall and how to resuscitate the complected international financial systems.

As would be expected, every G20 country in attendance brought its particular budgetary agenda to the table, looming world economic collapse aside. These partisan agendas naturally provoked the traditional petty in-fighting over special interests, huffy insinuations of "protectionism," and an intense desire to place the blame for this financial debacle on some Capital's doorsteps.

And it seemed many fingers were pointing West, as the chants resounded, "Blame America!"

What all the finger pointing failed to recognize, however, was that greed knows no borders.

Just ask the "Financial Fool's Day" rioters who filled London's streets, and angrily smashed in windows and ransacked bank lobbies, in protest of unbridled greed and executive bonuses. Or the Somali Pirates[1] who went on a spree during the first week of April and hijacked five more ships – to add to the other dozen they were already holding – in exchange for big ransom money.

---

[1] **SOMALIAN PIRATES:** The Somali Pirates and their highly lucrative ransom demands were a major threat to international shipping and boating off the Somalian peninsula/Horn of Africa during the war in Somalia from 2006 to 2009. Somalia was considered a failed state until 2012.

Or the French employees of 3M who held their manager hostage as protestors burned tires throughout Paris and marched on the presidential palace enraged over executive bonuses and golden parachutes[1] that the rioters themselves would never see as job losses mounted.

The international community didn't hesitate to jump on the big bull right beside America as it was charging forward, and every wild rider got to partake of the voracious financial windfalls with punch-drunk giddiness. Those intoxicating days have obviously left a very nasty hangover, and many of the international participants who enthusiastically shared in the boom-time have tried to cleverly maneuver toward absolution from the sin of greed by confessing innocent ignorance with the assertion that all fault rests with America; America made them do it.

Greed claims itself to be one of the seven deadly sins and even the root of all evil, yet to blame America for the greedy nature of mankind is as absurd as the parents of South Park, Colorado blaming Canada for the bad behavior of their children, even if they did win an Oscar for the song.

Today's global economic depression has cultivated a "class war" revolution of international proportions. On the surface, the communal revolts seem directed toward eradicating elitism and

---

[1] **BUSH FLU:** A highly resistant and uncooperative viral strain that was released from the golden parachutes strapped to the backs of financial district CEOs as they were ejected by their Board of Directors and pushed out of Air Force One. Subsequent studies eventually confirmed that the virus was carried and transmitted through the small air-borne drops of crude oil that leeched from the edges of the golden parachutes upon deployment. Symptoms include: Great Depression. No money in the bank. Your bank's ATM machine holds your debit card hostage and instead spits out a government I.O.U. by way of a receipt in the form of Federal Reserve Notes.

the redistribution of wealth, but underneath, simmering at the core, is rebellion against narcissism run amok.

The escalating worldwide working class resistance of today appears to possess some sort of unspoken consensus intent upon breaking the bonds of mental slavery propagated over time by Vulture Culture[1] and LAB-Rat[2] governing styles that are utterly disconnected and insulated from what's really happening on the ground.

---

[1] **VULTURE CULTURE** (A Cultural Mindset): The Vulture Culture is a parasitical cultural mindset that encourages self-serving individuals to collectively devour the flesh right off of the bones of society like a wake of New World Vultures gathering to feast on the susceptible. Those immersed in today's Vulture Culture tend to personify the gladiatorial spirit of "winner takes all;" and like the competitive arenas of ancient Rome where the sole objective of the properly indoctrinated gladiator is to win at any cost, every victory sustained is the direct result of cutthroat competition on steroids. There are no rules, there are no hostages. There is only winning. In this myopic quest to win, disciples of the Vulture Culture think nothing of pissing all over everything they step on, and the corrosive uric acid that rolls down their legs unchecked does little more than leave in its wake a wide trail of scorched earth. Those belonging to the Vulture Culture have absolutely no desire to contribute anything new or of value to the very society they feed on. They prefer instead to feed upon the remains of the day like scavengers, for what they lack in creative innovation, they make up for in carnage.

[2] **LAB-RAT** (Archetype): These are the fringe skulkers who hover just below the radar – like they're there but not really part of anything. They appear to be pleasant and normal and give the illusion of making some sort of contribution, yet underneath they're really cold fish with no true need for emotional substance or interpersonal depth. LAB-Rats navigate within a highly compartmentalized world that revolves solely around them which manifests itself in the form of brain-body incongruencies. It's almost as if some unseen master has strategically placed remote-controlled electronic stimulus patches all over their body and knows just when to trigger the switch. This brain-body disconnect gives them little instinct for even the most rudimentary consideration for the needs of another, resulting in a narcissistic drive to achieve their goals at any cost, without conscience or accountability. Busy scurrying and always on the go, and clearly no time for quiet introspection sans distraction, LAB-Rats can frequently be found flying the redeye from L.A. to Boston and back again with Blackberry in hand and a GPS perpetually connected to the unseen master. Evasive and duplicitous by nature, they might even tell you they live in France.

A world in chaos, fueled by widespread social turbulence without boundaries, provides a golden opportunity for the financial elite to move their resources and assets around virtually undetected. So where are the financial illuminatis quietly investing and sheltering their money now?

26

New Century Nurturing
May 4, 2009

While April may've popped out of March's Spring box like a Fool, May Day ushered in a new month filled with ancient traditions celebrating motherhood, fertility, and some light-hearted dancing around a Maypole.

Since history's beginning, the Mother archetype has been recognized as the creator and sustainer of life, the nurturer, the caregiver, and even the soft heart of humanity. Although science has attempted to create and grow human life within the confines of a sterile laboratory, the hard-wired role of suckling and socialization belongs to the Mother and the nurturer's influence has few limitations.

Today's challenging economic times and shriveling job markets have revealed an interesting paradigm shift where we've begun to see men outnumbering women in the loss of high paying jobs. This has resulted in women steadily becoming the household's primary breadwinner while more men remain at home to care for the family.

Familial units pulling together through troubled times is an admirable approach, yet with men increasingly playing a more substantial role on the home front, the country is beginning to rumble with the outcries of indignant male nurturers. The men who've dared to step into the important role of caregiver are now experiencing firsthand how thankless and invisible our society tends to perceive the function, so much so that many have even formed their own support groups.

To discount this paradigmatic transition as merely a movement toward the feminization of men would be unsound, since nurturing is gender neutral and essential for all humans, male and female, to flourish. Nurturing is the glue of any thriving civilization, and its existence, or non-existence, defines what that society will look like.

A culture that values the health and balanced well-being of its community finds it incumbent upon itself to recognize and support those who perform the necessary communal role of nurturer for it views nurturing as a form of preventative medicine. In contrast is the culture that believes nurturing to be a "give me," requiring little or no investment ... an approach that fosters nurturer burnout and outright neglect, with consequences most easily observed in an overflowing prison system.

We got a fleeting glimpse **in the rear view mirror** of Marion Robinson quietly moving into the White House after The Big BOPR's[1] inauguration. There were those who loudly argued the unnecessary expense to the nation of supporting a grandmother in the White House. The arguments unfortunately gave no consideration to the possibility that the hard costs of supporting Ms. Robinson in caring for her grandchildren could save us far more than the costs of a First Family neglected.

Sadly, in the red and black world of dollars and cents – coupled with the myopic belief that if it's invisible and intangible, it has little or no value and should therefore be free – the hue and cry about "letting Ms. Robinson move in" offered little mention of the great personal sacrifices this mother and grandmother has had to

---

[1] **THE BIG BOPR:** Barack Obama, President and "Renegade" (his Secret Service code name). He was the successor to President George W. Bush (aka XP "W") after being "sworn" in to office on January 20, 2009 as the 44th President of the United States of America, Inc. AKA Traitor 44.

make in order to provide a loving, stable environment for her family, as undervalued as that may seem in our bipolar American society.

With today's paradigm shift, the systemic adjustments now in progress are by no means limited to the overhaul of our economic and financial structures, but reverberate to include a significant realignment of our value systems as well. So what really costs society more: the true cost of nurturing or the true cost of neglect?

27

The Boyling Point
May 12, 2009

Andy Warhol's famous observations casually tossed like a bone to hungry paparazzi seem to be even more relevant in our real time, fast food world than they were when he quipped them nearly half a century ago.

Warhol believed, with good reason, that the mainstream media could enable anyone to achieve "instant" celebrity status whether they deserved it or not, even if that fame only lasted a fleeting 15 minutes – or until the media diverted the public's attention onto another shiny new object.

Today's carnivorous media can gobble up the raw and unseasoned with manufactured fame as soon as their prey has been blinded by the spotlight. Differing variations of the formula media blitz have been played out for the public's viewing pleasure time and again, where everyone can watch with morbid fascination as the wide-eyed deer in the spotlight is shamelessly fawned and fattened on praise before being publicly roasted and devoured on the spit.

And no meal ticket for the barbeque could ever be sold without the self-promoting Troll on the Bridge[1], since clearly, someone has

---

[1] **TROLL ON THE BRIDGE, or "TROLL" for short** (Archetype): These are the corporate-minded gatekeepers who block your every effort to maneuver around them and get across the bridge. This is occasionally done maliciously and without conscience, but more often than not, the blockade is enforced without the Troll even comprehending on a conscious level that it is "the hold-up" – the obstruction blocking all passage to the other side. Since Trolls often believe themselves infallible and eagerly seek to have that belief validated, they usually insist on some sort of ego caressing homage as payment before they'll finally

to take credit for luring that deer out of the forest, and then serve as the toll taker who shrewdly optimizes the deer's 15 minutes by selling as many tickets as possible.

With one look **in the rear view mirror** where objects may appear larger than they are, we realize the "15 minutes of fame" factor is simply a litmus test for staying power. Perhaps even a succinct way to separate those who've laid the foundation and worked with focused commitment toward a personal goal from those who have not, which can extend to include the wannabes and the could-bes.

No doubt media neophyte, Susan Boyle, has had a crash course in dog-eat-dog since her April 11, 2009 debut on "Britain's Got Talent," and her subsequent record-breaking YouTube viewings of the shockingly wonderful performance which firmly placed her name on the lips of the global population at a speed never before seen.

Sneering pre-performance assessments were conspicuously rendered by Ms. Boyle's talent judges, the audience, and even the world at large as all watched the frumpy, middle-aged, unemployed spinster courageously step out center stage in pursuit of her dream. (And to think, she would've been disqualified for being too old to perform on the "American Idol" version of the same show).

While over four decades of hard work and personal commitment obviously preceded that pivotal moment when Susan Boyle found herself "discovered," we find it difficult not to wonder if

---

step aside and let you pass them by. And as they smugly wallow in their self-induced position of power by being "the hold-up," Trolls are sadly ignorant to the unmistakable, yet ironic fact that they're usually standing in their own way and blocking their own progress as well.

there wasn't more to it than just luck and timing, for her pivotal moment resembled that of a "perfect storm" where each ingredient blended together at precisely the right moment to influence the destiny of all parties connected.

Only time will tell, if the decades of prep work Ms. Boyle invested in her craft will give her the staying power necessary to go beyond the proverbial 15 minutes of fame. But what we really want to know is what components must perfectly intersect and coalesce in order to create those fateful moments of manifestation?

28

Carnac The FMRI
July 4, 2009

As our industrialized nation and its citizens plummet ever deeper into debt and default, it's heartening to see behavioral masterminds fast at work discovering new ways to squeeze blood out of a turnip.

It seems no line exists today that a bill collector won't cross in its quest to wring payment from a distressed customer with a past due account. Evidence of this can be seen in the latest mass manipulation technique which involves the formulation of consumer psych profiles in order to diagnose individual lifestyle situations and preferences. These profiles are then extensively analyzed to determine how the information can be utilized and twisted to either emotionally extract payment or power market.

Should the reality of an unauthorized personal psychological profile not prove invasive enough, then perhaps it's time we let it all hang out in a world where our private inner thoughts are secretly scanned, catalogued and interpreted for future use and without our permission. Well, never fear, for Neuroscience has been busy in the background refining the art of mind reading with Functional Magnetic Resonance Imaging, or FMRI, research.

In the rear view mirror we saw an atom split to create a distinct fork in the road of providence. The high road of providence seemed illuminated and benevolent as it offered the prospect of an advanced energy source and the opportunity to improve quality of life for the masses on our planet Earth. The low road of providence, however, proved to be dark and sinister as its highway led promptly to the atomic bomb and the ability to render mass destruction in a fly-by. The bulk of the research money looks to have taken the low road.

This new wave neuro-technology has created another fork in the road of providence – a fork that cannot clearly offer an unobstructed view beyond the approaching horizon's blind spots. And like the potential of a split atom, the road taken will undoubtedly depend on the motivation and intention of those providing the essential research funding. Or as some would say, just follow the money.

To ponder the intricacies of merely one person's consciousness and the unique experiences that influence and form it, is mind boggling at best. The data now being compiled will ultimately require interpretation by some to-be-named professional qualified under some to-be-determined criteria, yet we wonder if it's possible to really anticipate the perceptions and true intentions deep within a human psyche.

It was funny when former late night talk show host Johnny Carson's "Carnac the Magnificent" knew the answers before the questions had even been asked partly because it had no true basis in our reality of the time. Funny how the humor begins to fade as we witness the present day reality of a rapidly compiled comprehensive thought identification data base, and the prospect of undisclosed powers believing they know the answers before the questions have even been asked.

In true Sci-Fi fashion and resembling that of contemporary attempts to block covert interceptions of private wireless phone conversations, we suspect few will be surprised to hear whispers of an underground movement actively employing counter-measures designed to block or jam involuntary random mind-reading scans on the ground.

How our thoughts are interpreted and how that information will be used to manipulate us in obscure ways is sufficiently disconcerting, but what we really want to know is who's going to own our minds and the thoughts it produces?

29

The Sopranos Return For Another Season on HMO
July 30, 2009

The Healthcare Insurance Reform Cicadas have risen once again after 16 years of underground silence.

The "Cicada HCIR" has shown itself to be a loud and highly irritating insect indigenous to the U-S-of-A since debuting in the 1940's when Harry S. Truman first cleared his throat with the annoying HCIR hum he'd picked up from his predecessor, Franklin D.

While insurance protection in every imaginable form is as old as mankind, it doesn't appear that modern day legislative regulation of the insurance industry has really influenced the hard core, down and dirty facets of the business overly much. And the most recent "Cicada HCIR" cyclical uprising has once again directed special attention toward the health insurance sector of the industry.

With all eyes now focused on the deficiencies in American healthcare coverage, we just couldn't resist one look **in the rear view mirror** to observe the approach of a black Lincoln Town Car with ebony tinted windows as it pulled along the curb and parked. The sedan's doors opened in unison and two piece-packing, black suited professionals sporting dark sunglasses stepped out onto the sidewalk with a job to do. The gangster collection agents were out in force to squeeze payment from the neighborhood in exchange for protection.

Strong arm collection styles are understandably believed by most to be outright extortion.

Nevertheless, there was a time long ago when buying this kind of insurance protection really meant buying protection, and the organization collecting premiums from the locals usually stood behind its protection promises because it kept out the competition and granted monopolized dominion over very valuable turf. The "organizzazione familia" naturally kept all premium payments collected as profit for there were no shareholders to share with, no underwriters, no exclusionary clauses for pre-existing conditions.

There's little question that the neighborhood had been made an offer it couldn't refuse. Paying up meant insurance coverage was in force. Payment not tendered when the hood collectors banked on having their palms greased resulted in premature end of life issues that were finished off with assertive euthanasia lacking in the customary compassion or compunction.

Like "The Godfather Insurance" days of yesteryear, there still remains an honor amongst thieves, and all honor goes to bottom line profits.

American health insurance policyholders have also been made an offer they can't refuse, except there's no one ensuring that the protections paid for and promised are actually being provided. Instead, top priority goes to substantially increasing shareholder profits which are dependent upon the number of claims not paid and policyholders being denied essential healthcare services.

If Al Capone had been running the health insurance racket for the last century, would the health industry be any different today?

30

Short Sighted
August 21, 2009

Regarded by many as the father of American literature, humorist Mark Twain once said, "Clothes make the man. Naked people have little or no influence in society."

20th century streakers sprinting through the '70's in nothing but their Nike jogging shoes undoubtedly had a different opinion, but it seems reasonable to expect that lifestyle and environmental demands would considerably influence what society deems fashionably suitable as we transition further into the 21st century.

When Michelle O. emerged from Air Force One in Arizona the other day, and catty commentary set the newswires ablaze as if the entire country had been sucked into the Grand Canyon, our **rear view mirror** conjured up an outtake from "Project Runway" we couldn't help but call, "First Lady on a Tarmac Catwalk."

France's first lady, Carla Bruni-Sarkozy, was perfection in a drab Dior ensemble, and as the outtake's featured commentator, we listened keenly as she melodiously described the fashion show's unfolding drama in her hallmark voice a la smolder. (We figure it's pretty safe to assume Madam Carla would disagree, like a true streaker would, with Mark Twain's "naked people" assertion, especially since her naked photos have been a favorite Christie's auction item of late).

The show's highlights included a fashion plate roundup of Michelle O. predecessors as they lined the tarmac catwalk before the first lady deplaned. Carla diplomatically described the summer vacation attire worn by those former first ladies in attendance:

Jackie O in Oleg Cassini capris, Gap T-Shirt, custom visored pill box hat, and peds with Keds.

Nancy Reagan shimmering in a one-shouldered Bill Blass sun dress (red, of course), sheer cover-up, and strappy sandals.

Hillary in jeans (to cover the cankles), yellow cotton blouse with matching shirt jacket, and Hush Puppies.

Laura Bush in a tailored ecru pantsuit, pink floral blouse, nude Spanx panty hose, and open toed Naturalizers.

The shot heard 'round the world must've backfired when Michelle O. finally stepped out onto the tarmac in hiking shorts, cream camisole with khaki overblouse, and workout tennies.

Given the media's reaction, you'd think Mr. Blackwell had turned over in his grave.

Our contemporary schitzo-media will undeniably go to great lengths to shear away anything akin to dignified boundaries in order to maintain a highly profitable double standard. All's fair as long as it sells, and it's clearly a two for one when it also stirs up a diversion from the doldrums of a boring summer.

Let it never be said that any self-serving mass media outlet ever rejected the opportunity to fill time and space with highly lucrative semi-nude and soft porn advertisements in the name of free press and capitalism, while simultaneously feigning outrage when the first "lady" has the audacity to expose her legs in hiking shorts while on holiday in triple-digit desert temps.

The fashion barometer once calibered by society's affluent does seem to be rapidly divesting alongside their depreciating balance sheets. Could it be that prevailing styles will begin to trend toward a life-in-the-real-world affordability making egalitarian standards more en vogue?

31

Mediocre Minds Think Alike
September 4, 2009

The 1894 legislation making Labor Day a national holiday essentially worked out to be a hasty bureaucratic effort to appease American labor forces after the militia opened fire on striking railroad workers in the Midwest. Few today, however, would expect that bit of ancient history to influence procession motifs along the nation's holiday parade routes.

For many contemporary Americans, Labor Day is simply considered the symbolic end of summer, and a day of rest from the laborious task of looking for a new job.

For those a little more prone to introspection, this legislated day of rest can offer pause for reflection about what sort of creative approach might be needed these days in order to secure substantial and sustainable employment during the festerings of a chronic corporate dumb down overrun with mediocrity.

When the bar is never set above mediocre, it's quite easy to be lulled into a false sense of competence ... until one is downsized, that is.

Truth is, consistent guidelines and standards that support an entire organization as its staff works toward a common and (hopefully) profitable purpose are not only necessary, but can be mutually beneficial as well.

Obviously, balance and common sense haven't always prevailed. Too many rules and suppressive regulations imposed by corporate brass onto its workforce have served not only to firmly secure the power held by those making the rules (since they are typically the exception to the rules), but appear to be the inspiration behind the mediocre brainstorming that has filled corporate think tanks across the board.

Hollywood satirists have yet to fail in scripting profound dialogue that truly mirrors this anomaly of corporate culture in a way that ironically makes us laugh about it.

We laughed when Jim from "The Office" said, "I've always subscribed to the idea that if you really want to impress your boss, you go in there and you do mediocre work, half-heartedly."

We also laughed in "Big" when Jon Lovitz's "Scotty" said to Tom Hanks' "Josh," "Listen, what are you trying to do? Get us all fired? You gotta slow down. Pace Yourself."

The propagation of modern day mediocrity has unconventionally integrated old world Machiavellian principles to cultivate a corporate "crab bucket" mentality in the workplace. Sure we'd all like to see our friends and colleagues get ahead, but not too far ahead. So we work hard to never outshine our corporate comrades lest we forget that the tallest blade of grass is the first to get cut. And those clutching the ladder's top rung continue to rule with little concern for those clinging to the bottom rung, for those at the bottom are too busy taking each other out vying for a better position to ever challenge the powers roosting at the top.

We looked **in the rear view mirror** while listening to our iPod and watched the CEOs of the music industry spin 78 RPMs as they whirled to preserve their dominion when creative technology began to weaken their syndicated stronghold. Amazingly, instead of spending their billions on competitive innovation and integration, they chose to invest their dollars in litigation to halt the progress and then try to control it. Perhaps they thought they were too big to fail and didn't need to keep up. Or maybe they just believed the surrounding corporate yes-men spawned out of mediocrity who routinely tickled their executive ears with disconnected reinforcement.

And the music industry clearly isn't the only industry reeling from the limitations inherent with mediocrity, for mediocrity and creative innovation are incompatible co-workers.

Albert Einstein's belief that "great spirits have always encountered violent opposition from mediocre minds" would rarely find a true innovator and creative thinker in disagreement. So does this mean that when we hit a blockade résistance from the prevailing Lemming-Groupthink majority, then maybe we're really on to something?

32

Wait Weight
September 18, 2009

The times they are a-changin', and America's double helping of new century change has stimulated its population to TARP[1] their tears away three times a day with take-out. True capitalists know that when it comes down to the emotional buttons pushed by recession and social depression, there's little a super-sized, super-value menu can't fix.

Nothing like a severe economic downturn, no paycheck, and a heap of recession depression to tempt even the heartiest of weight watchers with the promise of an extra-large, cheap meal offering little but a week's worth of empty calories in one sitting and high cholesterol. The fact that cultural perceptions about food consumption have shifted (to the delight of advertisers) from healthy sustenance to an emotionally needy pastime hasn't helped either.

High speed technological advancements have obviously changed the way we work and play as well. One side effect of this change has been society's overall devaluation of basic social skills and interpersonal connection. The ensuing social retardation, and the isolation and loneliness it begets, goes a long way toward creating a void that only sugar, fat, salt, and lots of sense-assaulting noisy stimulation can fill.

---

[1] **TARP** (Troubled Asset Relief Program) is a direct result of the Emergency Economic Stabilization Act of October, 2008 (aka "Bank Bailout of 2008" and "Wall Street Bailout") enacted by President George W. Bush which allowed the U.S. government to use taxpayer funds to the tune of $700 Billion to purchase toxic assets and equity from failing banks/financial institutions in order to prop up and prevent a total financial sector collapse said to be due in part to the subprime mortgage crisis.

Upon heavy reflection **in the rear view mirror** we couldn't help but see that extra-large "Closed for Repairs" sign hanging on the entrance gate of Disneyland's "It's a Small World" attraction for the good part of a year.

Originally designed in the 1960's, the ride was unquestionably in need of some 21st century updating. The sense of urgency prompting 2008's closure, however, seems to have sprang from a chronic dilemma that even strategic rider placement couldn't resolve; namely, the ride's fiberglass boats were routinely bottoming out on cellulite sandbars and protruding paunches, thereupon bringing the entire ride to a constipated standstill. Logically, swift removal of the damming girth from the grounded lead boat was the sole remedy for restoring the ride to a normal flow.

With this recurring delay in passage came the certain knowledge that our world wasn't so small after all.

While Disneyland eventually got around to dredging the plus-sized waterways it needed to accommodate the bulk of Americans, newfangled stadium movie theaters were long in the game with a "build it and they will come" approach to larger cushy seats, king-size cup holders and mega-sized buckets of popcorn that any properly stocked self-service condiment counter could help saturate in buttery flavored grease.

Hollywood then hit a homerun by offering more to love in casting plenty of big screen super (sized) stars who delivered body image peace of mind to movie goers as they pac-manned their way through the raisinettes and the previews.

In an era of survival aero-mergers, the airline industry has taken a more tightening-of-the-seatbelt approach to the expanding

American waistline. Weight restrictions aside, the more seats crammed on to an aircraft, the more tickets to be sold. No one cares whose roly polys onto whom. Instead of enticing passengers to fly with the promise of a comfy seat and airy comfort food, they just stopped feeding everyone altogether. Everyone except perhaps the growing number of highly stressed, plump pilots who hold our lives in their hands at cruising altitudes (and are severely under-compensated for it when considering their liability), yet look like a heart attack waiting to happen when the plane is parked at the gate.

Time has always been of the essence, but anymore, time is just a mcflurry in our world of instant gratification at the speed of a search engine set to find "now fast," "a lot a deal," and "cheap free."

Yet, when it comes down to the fundamental task of feeding our bodies, we suspect if one were to simply practice a slower more nutritious approach to dining – or to wait – odds are the load will become lighter, both emotionally and physically. And conversely, to habitually gulp down fast food on the go – or to not wait – odds are the load will end up much heavier all the way around.

It would appear excuses hold little weight when personal prerogative gives us permission to prioritize the time we need to properly nourish our bodies, for in the end, we alone are physically accountable for what we put into our mouths.

A very weighty issue indeed, but what we really want to know is how do you weigh in? And what are you waiting for?

33

Faux Food
October 7, 2009

Another summer has ended, and our nation's school children have returned to their classrooms thanks to the old agrarian calendar. While the school year may continue its primitive revolution around the seasonal till and harvest, few are the children who have personally beheld the phenomenon of fertile farmland, let alone worked in the fields at harvest time.

Although many of our children will probably never participate directly in the hands-on science of crop cultivation, most are taught in science class about a very fundamental part of the Earth's ecosystem called the food chain. A grade school science lesson on the food chain teaches us how energy flows from one level of existence to another upon consumption; and since food is energy, every living creature in the food chain gets its energy from the food it eats.

Naturally, combining food chain principles with proverbial wisdom never fails to yield the ever popular, "You are what you eat." Nutritionists have been preaching these timeless words of warning for centuries (and so has the Catholic Church with its Eucharist for that matter, but contrary to parishioner belief, the church isn't part of the Earth's ecosystem).

The irrefutable science supporting the importance of a balanced ecosystem prompts us to question the motives of Big Food (and the reason behind government farm subsidies) when we consider the methodical alterations being perpetrated upon the natural flow of our food chain.

Foods today are described as processed, fabricated, artificial, and synthetic; and are full of chemical flavorings, artificial color, preservatives, fillers and binders as if this is normal. Even our basic staples like sugar and flour are known to be bleached, processed and refined. And let's not overlook the customary corn syrup and casein infusions found in most things prepared and pre-packaged for human consumption.

Perhaps the reason we eat three times more than we should is because we're unable to get the nutrients our bodies need from the foods we're eating and consequently, we never truly feel full or satisfied. Grade school science reminds us that it's impossible to get life sustaining nutrients from something that is not alive and a natural part of the food chain.

We had a flashback **in the rear view mirror** that made us gasp in horror right alongside Charleton Heston as we watched a long line of waste disposal trucks pull up behind the Soylent processing plant, and proceed to dump one cargo of corpses after another. After the dead meat was delivered and then cleverly reconstituted into Soylent green wafers, we could only gag when the recycle of life was fed to an unsuspecting and hungry population of 2022.

To dismiss "Soylent Green" as just some old 1973 dystopian sci-fi flick that couldn't possibly have any relevance to our 2009 reality seems logical. Surely everyone knows that only in the movies would people be dumb enough to fall for a corporate gorilla marketing campaign designed to convince them that Soylent green was a nutritious processed food made from high-energy plankton, and something they couldn't live without.

Well, no one ever said that truth in advertising standards actually require anyone to tell the whole truth, and nothing but the truth.

Far from it, for standard marketing practices make it a point to routinely stretch and manipulate the illusion of truth for maximum profitability. Any detrimental consumer side effects are usually considered negligible when measured against bottom line profit margins.

Case in point offers us a **side mirror view** at the marketing strategy for a popular brand of sucralose, and how its no-calorie sweetener is a better alternative to real sugar. The product slogan rationally asserts, "it starts with sugar, it tastes like sugar, but it's not sugar." What is never disclosed in plain speak, however, is that this artificial sweetener is basically chlorinated table sugar, and after intensive chemical processing, took what began as natural and made it unnatural.

An appeal to our collective need for sweetness without caloric consequences or accountability makes it a profitable marketing triumph, and the masses have been properly convinced that real sugar is bad and artificial sweeteners are good.

Corporate capitalism shamelessly intent upon increasing profits without a conscience has worked hard behind the scenes to remote control every facet of contemporary life. This clearly includes what we're being fed, on every level.

Our supermarket shelves and delicatessen counters are being stocked daily with tasty mystery foods – foods consisting of unknowable and unnatural ingredients that are incongruent with the very food chain ecosystem we are an integral part of. We suspect changes in the lucrative business of reconstituting food will not be forthcoming from Big Food any time soon. Not until, of course, it gets outed like Big Tobacco did. Until then, caveat emptor – let the buyer beware.

So will the cumulative effects of consuming nothing but faux food eventually turn us all into mannequins?

34

Apple Pie Goes Rogue
November 17, 2009

Facebook was the tactical wall from which the contagious propaganda was hawked and sneezed into the atmosphere, and Twitter kept the infectious buzz spreading like the H1N1 virus in real time. It only took four months of gimmicky posts and tweets to prime every true American for the debut of a new grassroots animated reality show aptly named, "Back Asswards."

"Back Asswards" – featuring former Alaska governor and 2008 GOP Vice Presidential candidate, Sarah Palin[1], in the 15 minute role of a lifetime – finally premiered this week with award winning drama and the usual dysfunctional media frenzy.

The leading "Voice of No" who chimes with the times with one finger on the pulse of ordinary American folks everywhere has made us believe she's found her calling. And in her role as the new flag waving "Fresh Breeze of Toon Town," there's little doubt the year 2012 will yield much more than merely the climactic end of the Mayan calendar.

Speculation has predictably swirled around whether or not her future will include a run for the 2012 GOP Presidential nomination, especially after Mrs. Quit dubiously resigned her Alaskan governorship in July. Considering what the GOP has to

---

[1] **SARAH PALIN**: Palin was the former Governor of Alaska from 2006 until 2009, when she resigned before finishing her term. She was the 2008 VP running mate of Republican Presidential candidate, John McCain. Palin had a reputation for making up words during her speeches, and often referred to herself as a Maverick, a Rogue, a Ronald Reagan devotee, and sometimes as a "Pitbull with Lipstick" when at hockey games. She also claimed that she could see Russia from her house.

pick from these days, however, it looks as if the answer to the speculations would be a resounding, "You betcha!"

Nothing screams, "I can lead America," louder than a tell-all, fact flawed autobiography without an index.

When right went wrong was when we realized that this all-knowing hockey mom was in desperate need of some common sense solutions if she really wanted to win the next big race, and her campaign handlers must be fully capable of finishing up all that she starts but only gets half way through.

Fellow conservative, Elizabeth Hasselbeck, would undoubtedly be an excellent choice for the role of campaign press secretary. Not only would it be refreshing for her to work with another beautiful woman whose views are just as black and white with no shades of gray, but here was a seasoned media personality who could offer some common sense solutions for reconnecting with the liberal media outlets that were unfriended by the "Rogue Gone Social Networker."

Another common sense solution to her challenges with the press might include recruiting Tina Fey to act as a stand-in for all press conferences and interviews. That way she could personally bypass all of those pesky news anchors asking all of those annoying questions. Of course, in order to keep it real, she'd need to continue writing and delivering her own entertaining off-message, wandering around the bend speeches going nowhere, chock full of clichés, one-liner sound bites, new Hillbilly vocabulary words, and folks appeal.

Then there's Levi Johnston (aka Ricky Hollywood and Bristol's baby daddy). We don't expect he'll be going away any time soon, especially since he's considered part of the family. Just because he's a high school drop-out doesn't mean he's stupid, for he apparently proved himself to be a quick study in American capitalism during his time behind the scenes on the last campaign trail. One conservative common sense solution to reigning in this morally lost young man would be to bring on board another former beauty queen, Carrie Prejean[1], to act as Levi's moral compass. And if we're lucky, maybe Prejean's own drama will overshadow Levi's limelight.

We found our eyes glazing over as we glanced **in the rear view mirror** while listening to "Mother Maverick" on the radio during her interview with Rush Limbaugh[2]. When the right-right twins finished discussing her new substantive book on policy, we were left scratching our heads, yet hungering for more.

While fact checking doesn't seem to be at the top of the list for either Palin or Limbaugh, deep dark secrets are. So when the GOP GILF starts down the 2012 campaign trail where every skeleton hiding in the closet will become a headline, we'll be standing by, waiting for something truly sensational, like Sarah Palin is really the illegitimate sister of Rush Limbaugh.

As for the lazy media, the beauty queen "Bering to set the record Strait" is as irresistible as fast food. She serves it up fast and easy like a drive-thru window, and few are the professionals who take the time to research what they're eating before regurgitating it out

---

[1] **CARRIE PREJEAN**: Prejean was a model, former Miss California USA 2009 beauty queen, and Miss USA 2009 first runner up. She was stripped of her Miss California USA crown for breach of contract after a partially nude "modeling" photograph of her appeared on a celebrity gossip blog. Ensuing litigation later unveiled a home video "sex tape."

[2] **RUSH LIMBAUGH**: Limbaugh was an opinionated, loud and outspoken American conservative political commentator who hosted "The Rush Limbaugh Show" radio show from 1988 until his death in 2021. He was arrested for prescription drug fraud in 2006 due, in part, to his addiction to painkillers; OxyContin being a particular favorite.

for worldly consumption. And not unlike a fast food meal which deceives us into believing our bellies are full, we're essentially left starving for true nourishment and bloated with gas barely an hour later.

Love it or hate it, no presidential campaign has ever been won without support from the media, and no exceptions for going rogue or being mavericky either. Perhaps inviting Hillary over for a cup of coffee will help to clean up her relationship with the press in time for season two of "Back Asswards – Kissing Babies." Even pit bulls wearing lipstick still have to twist and contort in order to lick themselves clean.

But what we really want to know is do we all have to watch?

35

Cashing In On COIN
December 19, 2009

Right about the time Erik Prince of Blackwater-now-Xe[1] was sagaciously gray-mailing the U.S. government with an exposé in "Vanity Fair," and Osama Bin Laden was shrewdly recruiting a fresh round of terrorists from American soil, we were furiously working at our laptops hunting the internet for some practical financial advice in a feeble attempt at damage control as the economy continues its slippery downward slope.

Following a trail of click-through links, we inadvertently stumbled upon a website that resembled an online scavenger hunt called "Find the COIN."

They say the best place to hide something is in plain sight, and "Find the COIN" was clearly counting on it. First glance gave the impression of top secret encrypted access only, yet we were able to navigate the user-friendly site with the ease customary of any other public domain. It took only minutes to discover that the two adversaries pitted against each other in this virtual scavenger hunt were none other than Erik Prince and Osama Bin Laden themselves, using the avatars FLY and CHAMELEON, respectively.

The grand prize was a hunting trip with Dick Cheney while camping with al-Qaeda in the heart of the Swat Valley. Given the

---

[1] **BLACKWATER**: Blackwater Worldwide was an American military contractor (mercenary army) founded by Erik Prince who was a Navy SEAL and CIA asset. It was reputed to be VP Dick Cheney's mercenary army of choice during the Bush Administration from 2001 to 2008. Blackwater changed its name to Xe in 2009.

scavenger map they had to work with (shown below), it was obvious there could never be a winner.

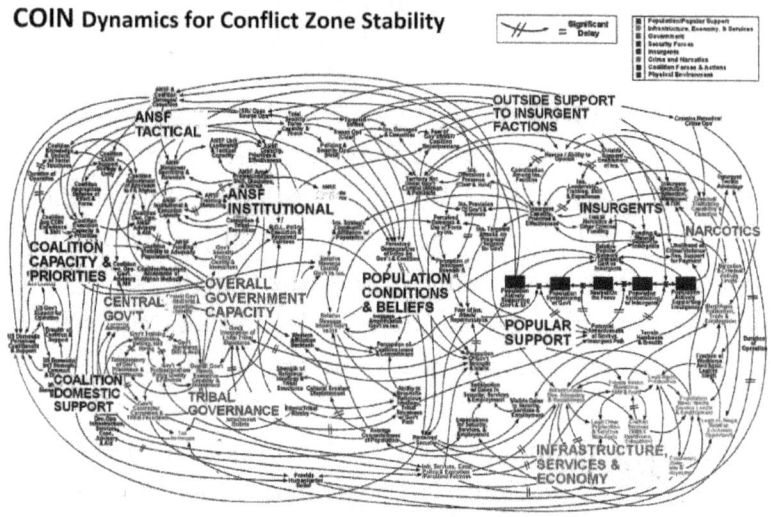

Copyright Disclaimer under Section 107 of the Copyright Act of 1976. Allowance is made for "fair use" for purposes such as commentary, criticism, teaching, education, parody, comedy, research and news reporting.

COIN = Counterinsurgency Dynamics

The site permitted us to seamlessly trace their high-tech/low-tech maneuvers across the scavenger hunt's mapped out terrain where the opponents' choreographed war dance was being destructively played out on an expansive international stage – all orchestrated to the beat of technology's rap song.

The CHAMELEON's right-sided domination of the scavenger map looked to be absolute, as did the FLY's left-handed supremacy. It appeared that CHAMELEON's strategic preference was the aggressive accumulation of powerful modems and the equipment necessary to post YouTube recruiting promos, instruction videos, and the occasional "catch me if you can" taunts to FLY across his Facebook wall.

The FLY, on the other hand, had left a furious trail of snatch-and-grab tweets posting classified coordinates for strategic assassination targets. More interested in acquiring beefier helicopters than potent modems, FLY seemed intent upon fully implementing his 3-F systematic action plan: FIND the target, FIX the target's routine and FINISH the target off ... all directed, of course, at 3-F-ing CHAMELEON.

A glance **in the rear view mirror** offered us a crystal ball reflection of the Land of Oz as the Wicked Witch of the West cast her sleeping spell upon the expansive poppy fields that blanketed the yellow brick road on the way to the Emerald City. Doubtless few would rush to compare the Helmand province of Afghanistan to the Land of Oz, yet few will deny that the road leading out of Helmand's poppy fields is indubitably made of golden bricks. And somewhere over that rainbow is a pot of gold used to fund world chaos and conflict as the masses close their sleepy eyes to the underlying machinations of the true power brokers.

Deep Throat knew what he was talking about when he urged us to follow the money, for the one who controls the money is believed to control the world because money makes the world go 'round. A simplified version of doing the math might look something like this: Money = Power = More Money.

Yes, there will always be plenty of money to be made by the robber barons hard at work sparking civil dissention and provisioning war zones by supplying both sides with what they need to keep the sparks flying. Another thing's for certain too, there'll always be a need for an evil Boogey Man antagonist to pit the perception of good against.

World domination through cash control is an ageless game. Wouldn't then a declaration of war against evil be an illusion that simply makes the rich richer and allows us to feel good about it?

36

Looking The Part
January 12, 2010

2009's last call had us optimistically humming "Auld Lang Syne" right along with the other merrymakers who also couldn't afford to attend Tavern on the Green's last supper in Central Park. When the clock chimed in at midnight, we briskly donned our 3-D glasses looking for an exclusive preview of the year 2010 from the land of the beautiful people.

Those first impressions overpowered our senses with panoramic images so vibrant and aesthetically alluring, we were momentarily convinced that perfection was attainable. Although the sweeping images were specifically designed to entice on the surface, we realized upon second glance that they were, in fact, highly flawed, for they were either flush with gaping holes formerly plumped up with body parts, or sprouting extra parts like Lakshmi with add-ons.

Nothing was as it seemed, and evidently nothing can make the unattainable attainable faster than the magic wand of Photoshop.

Peering **in the rear view mirror** allowed us to reflect upon a time when skilled artisans offered up credible representations of life in the real world. Whether these representations were designed with fabric to be worn as fashion, or masterfully painted on canvas as a depiction of emerging social modulations, or memorialized through the lens of a camera; the imagery was authentic and the camera never lied.

In the process of immortalizing the life and times around them, artistic historians have oftentimes been called visionary, even ahead of their time. And while Salvador Dali may've been considered ahead of his time during the 1930's, we're pretty sure he never expected one modern day interpretation of his "Soft Construction with Boiled Beans (Premonition of Civil War)" to include the place where body parts become art after they've been Photoshop cropped in the hasty pursuit of manipulated perfection.

Civilization overall has gleaned innumerable advantages from the technological advancements of the last decade, and nothing quenches the inherent human need for instant gratification faster than output with a keystroke. Unfortunately, something is lost in this pursuit of instant outcome, and the experienced would call it quality.

There are those who maintain "life is a journey, not a destination." This philosophical expression seems to suggest that life's greatest value is realized through an accumulation of experiences that stimulate internal growth and development, and not in the concluding moments at final breath. The scientific community apparently concurs with a comparable axiom of its own in "the joy of physics isn't in the results, but in the search itself."

We call this process vs. product, or perhaps just another way to extol the virtues of learning long division.

Today's technology has made readily available the tools necessary to efficiently manipulate our external mask to conform in a click with the fickle and fleeting version of what is considered desirable in the eyes of advertisers. Whether it be unrealistic or physically unattainable is irrelevant because within a smartphone lies the power to virtually redefine reality and create an alternate world of our own design that is inhabited by fantastic representations of our alter ego.

Yet, no matter how much we virtually alter our reality, certain truths remain self-evident; namely, "where ever you go, there you are."

As instant product output continues to override the patient investment true quality demands, could it be that quality too is in the process of being virtually redefined?

37

Seeing Double
February 24, 2010

That annual day of love affectionately known half the world over as Valentine's Day saw the other half of the globe celebrating the Lunar New Year as it ushered in the "Year of the Tiger" with hopes of good fortune. All of this luck in love hoopla gave us pause to wonder what lovers and tigers could possibly have in common.

It's said that the Year of the Iron Tiger (or is that the "9-Iron Tiger?") will keep away the three main tragedies of any household, and we can only surmise those averted tragedies would include something like NOT:

1.   Carelessly driving the family SUV into a tree at the end of the driveway in the wee hours of Thanksgiving night;

2.   Discovering extracurricular texts and phone calls from strange women on your husband's cell phone; and

3.   Being forced to fend off a paparazzi feeding frenzy.

In with the Tiger also comes the superstitious belief that the year won't be a good one for getting married. No one probably knows this better than the Arab ambassador who was treated to a cross-eyed view of marriage on his wedding day in Cairo a couple of weeks ago. We assume the bearded bride didn't marry a hairless man, but there was obviously only room for one beard in that household. After Mr. Ambassador cried foul and obtained a hasty annulment, all we could see **in the rear view mirror** was burning rubber when he hotfooted out of town with no booty in the back.

Mr. Ambassador's desire to have it both ways evidently backfired when the truth was unveiled, much to his (very public) humiliation. The discarded wife, however, incontestably landed on her feet financially thanks to his $136,000 endowment. Perhaps the Lunar New Year should've been called the Year of the Tigress instead.

The anthropology deeply nestled within the species homo sapien has proven itself to be hard wired into the most basic male-female interchange. Few would argue that the human male tends to gravitate towards visually attractive women who can reproduce, just as the female tends to gravitate towards strong men who can provide and protect. While the delicate balance of power between the genders has been historically lopsided in favor of the dominant male, it appears the pendulum has begun to swing in the direction of the educated female.

And it looks as if this shift is about to give new meaning to the phrase "double standard."

As the economic advantages once commanded by men continues to decline in favor of breadwinning women, traditional roles have logically begun to alter as well. Yet, somewhere within this shift in financial power percolates a healthy opportunity to incorporate these evolving standards and redefine the contributions each partner is expected to make to the partnership.

Replacing some of that old anthropological hard wiring has undeniably shown itself to be a challenge for today's men and women as they both struggle to find a new normal in contemporary society. How then will the institution of marriage ultimately be redefined, and will it stand the test of time?

38

POTUS, Inc.
March 30, 2010

We weren't really sure if the Moon was in the seventh house, or if Jupiter was aligned with Mars when the Sun transitioned into Aquarius in January, but what we do know is that a new age began with surprisingly little fanfare and very few outcries from an indignant American public.

Perhaps that's because there was little the people could do about the "Citizens United" decision made behind those closed Supreme Court doors where our nine Justices sequestered themselves away from prying eyes and inquiring human minds. The four judicial voices of dissent who did speak out with some sort of conscience were simply not enough, for ultimately the majority overruled. And the highest court in the land has spoken, with no room for debate.

This un-appealable overruling has, for all intents and purposes, removed the constitutional distinction that once separated the human being (previously considered the citizenry and heartbeat of America) from the inorganic corporate entity.

Of course, our Chief Justice was quick to smooth it all over with First Amendment and freedom of speech references by way of attempt to defend the court's prejudiced activism in deciding to decide on something it wasn't necessarily even asked to decide on.

Jubilance justifiably overflows for every large corporation of American birth that strategically envisions this landmark ruling to be their special interest way of leveling the playing field, and it isn't hard to guess whose playing field will be leveled.

So now that the days of hiding behind the corporate veil are over, the big guns can openly come out of the closet with their stockpiles while mobilizing a coordinated invasion of the 2012 presidential elections ... and just in time for the Mayan calendar to end. Frankly, we were rendered speechless when we began to envision the impending 2012 electoral process, and just how the American road to rulership might be navigated and capitalized.

We have every reason to believe that the campaign trail will begin predictably with the usual mannerisms: a welcoming gesture of open arms extending toward empty, upturned palms looking to be filled. Few will be shocked when the "Party of No" begins to briskly change its song to "Yes!Yes!Yes!" with the fevered pitch that only unfettered corporate financing can inspire. The GOP won't be singing alone, however, for in this joint fund-raising venture, true bipartisanship will prevail like never before.

As the clock starts to wind down on whatever remains of "Mother Maverick's[1]" 15 minutes, the GOP will bloat with confidence as it swiftly moves to back a new heavyweight candidate guaranteed to sweep every primary, win the election by a landslide, and then move the Oval Office to the winner's corporate headquarters in Arkansas.

---

[1] **SARAH PALIN:** Palin was the former Governor of Alaska from 2006 until 2009, when she resigned before finishing her term. She was the 2008 VP running mate of Republican Presidential candidate, John McCain. Palin had a reputation for making up words during her speeches, and often referred to herself as a Maverick, a Rogue, a Ronald Reagan devotee, and sometimes as a "Pitbull with Lipstick" when at hockey games. She also claimed that she could see Russia from her house.

Decades of successful corporate branding has already placed the familiar name of our next president, "Wally Mart, Inc." firmly upon the lips of the American population. And Wally Mart, Inc. will deeply touch the hearts of America even further with its sentimental, oldie but goodie campaign slogan: "Uncle Sam Wants You!"

Since Wally Mart, Inc. currently has long standing co-dependent economic arrangements with China (and our military), it will logically super-size its campaign platform with class-defining promises of privatizing profits so its corporate comrades can grow richer, and socializing risk so all of the financial burdens can be carried on the hard working backs of the American people. This agenda will not only clear the way to economize by centralizing distribution, it'll create thousands of low paying American jobs, and the masses will be kept so busy producing cheap goods and knock offs that they won't have time to think about anything other than survival.

Easily locating Wally Mart, Inc.'s corporate charter from 1962 will not only substantiate its American birth, but prove beyond question that the corporation exceeds the Constitutional 35-year age minimum. **In the rear view mirror** we can see the country being seduced by convincing election commercials romanticizing Wally Mart, Inc.'s humble mid-western beginnings while selling kitsch back in the 1950's.

As the first corporation to be selected President of the United States (POTUS), Wally Mart, Inc. proudly displays its "Inc." designation as if it were a PhD. Upon inauguration, Wally Mart, Inc. will undoubtedly take suffragistic steps to grant all corporations the right to vote, whilst proceeding to fill every seat in the House and Senate with corporate America, thereby cutting out the middle man.

It appears the scales of American justice have been unequivocally tipped in favor of the supreme corporation with deep pockets. What's next? Robots take over the world?

39

Pomp and Promises
April 16, 2010

The end of the school year is fast approaching. With this ending comes the beginning of an off-campus chapter in the lives of thousands of university students who have completed their core curriculums, and are now ready to enter the realm of the educated professional with freshly printed diplomas and loads of academic debt clamoring for repayment.

By the time their alma mater marching bands get around to stepping up the "Pomp and Circumstance" rehearsal schedules, most of the eligible graduates will have already been fitted for cap and gown, and be intently focused on the hunt for post-graduation employment in a paid position that even remotely corresponds with their chosen fields of study.

For the graduating majority who were assured that a college education would be an investment in their future fulfillment, and well worth the expense and resultant debt load, the job pickins are slim.

A sign-of-the-times reality check can be readily found with any routine sweep of the circulated job postings on the more "reputable" employer job boards over the last several years. Naturally, many large employers listing positions to be filled have unabashedly demonstrated their intentions of turning today's economic lemons into profitable lemonade through unpaid internships. The approach is avariciously rationalized when one considers the trade off – educated slave labor in exchange for dangled promises of a long-term position that eventually pays, maybe.

As the nation's unemployment rate continues to realistically hover in the double-digits and still neglect to reflect the real time stats of the severely under-employed, we can't help but wonder what our lettered citizens are expected to do with their education and expensive training ... especially now that the Census Bureau has all of the doctorate-to-door census taking temps it can handle.

When it came time for us to be counted, it came with a hard knock at the door, followed by a hard look **in the rear view mirror** that put us back on the revolutionary road of the 1960's where we could compare the indelible skid mark the '60's social revolution left on society with the financial revolution that is currently underway.

The 1960's unquestionably saw a collective insurgency that ultimately dismantled the traditional and established social structures which were perceived to be oppressive and limiting. To conform to the expectations set forth by the "establishment" was to have individuality suppressed by those standards, and personal freedoms unacceptably confined. For many the answer was to simply drop out; drop out of college, drop out of society, fall off the grid.

Today's financial revolution, however, seems to be rooted in financial oppression and the subjugation that comes with financial slavery. If society as a whole can no longer be effectively manipulated to submit and conform through fear of communal ostracism, then apparently it can be shackled and whipped into submission through heavy debt. Yet, instead of dropping out, the revolutionaries of today truly want to contribute to our GDP, and have literally bought into the belief that higher education is their way to a secure future.

Consequently, too many have now been left burdened with unmanageable debt and no job to show for it.

The United States of America, Inc. has certainly not been immune to the shackles of heavy national debt either; nevertheless, its corporate children appear to have openly abandoned the needs of their Motherland while hiding behind the veil of "free market capitalism," now that they've all been bailed out of course.

Once again the discord between corporate America and her U.S. Mother is being publicly waged at the expense of the people. While corporate America loudly whines on about how it just can't seem to find qualified domestic workers in order to justify its outsourcing cheap labor from abroad, Mother America takes her corporate children to task with accusations of unpaid intern abuses under the guise of federal labor law violations. In the end, all accounting points to payroll tax dollars – corporate America doesn't want the payables, and America's Treasury wants the receivables.

All speculation now goes to how the newly-educated, over-educated, unemployed and under-employed will find new income opportunities during the transition.

Clearly not motivated enough to create quality domestic jobs at this point in the revolution, corporate America continues to blatantly exploit the fresh ideas and innovative concepts of the vulnerable without paying for any of it. It reminds us of an old saying, "Why should they buy the cow when they can get the milk for free?"

40

Trolling For Transparency
May 2, 2010

We're not sure what's worse – having to learn about something we never thought we needed to know, or coming to grips with the verifiable truth that our private pursuits are being systematically archived for future use against us.

As corporate America continues to tighten its chokehold on the nation's workforce by installing a battalion of Trolls on every Bridge[1], we're getting a crash course in what publicists have known all along; namely, managing our public image is a full time job.

In the rear view mirror we saw a time, not very long ago, when an impressive resume', written referral letters and a great personal interview would reward those in search of suitable employment with a hired position commensurate with education and experience. The times, however, are clearly a-changin', because what we see now are invasive corporate Trolls making damaging judgment calls based solely upon an applicant's on-line social life ... and oftentimes without even confirming that the

---

[1] **TROLL ON THE BRIDGE, or "TROLL" for short** (Archetype): These are the corporate-minded gatekeepers who block your every effort to maneuver around them and get across the bridge. This is occasionally done maliciously and without conscience, but more often than not, the blockade is enforced without the Troll even comprehending on a conscious level that it is "the hold-up" – the obstruction blocking all passage to the other side. Since Trolls often believe themselves infallible and eagerly seek to have that belief validated, they usually insist on some sort of ego caressing homage as payment before they'll finally step aside and let you pass them by. And as they smugly wallow in their self-induced position of power by being "the hold-up," Trolls are sadly ignorant to the unmistakable, yet ironic fact that they're usually standing in their own way and blocking their own progress as well.

screened profile under review actually belongs to the applicant, and not to some random unknown who just happens to have a similar name.

While contemporary society works hard to exonerate its dark side by pretending the shadow doesn't exist, corporate America is busy working in the shadows trying to sustain a hypocritical double standard of "full transparency." This shady approach has not only created a unilateral opportunity for the corporations making all of the rules to micro-manage every worker's life under the pretense of smart business, it has also given its Trolls the power to kick off of the bridge any poor wretch who has the misfortune of being virtually connected to the wrong "friend."

Now that we know that we need good credit in order to get the very job that we need to get the good credit, and that we'll be indiscriminately judged guilty by association for connections with the wrong "friends" (as may be arbitrarily determined by any Troll working the Bridge), we now know that it's time we take charge of our virtual, and very public, persona.

Well, "WhoIs" may claim to provide an identity for everyone, but the new beta "WhoIsMiniMe" has set its user-friendly platform up to provide the perfect virtual image for everyone.

"WhoIsMiniMe" heralds itself to be the foolproof virtual PR platform from which to launch your own personal publicity campaign. "WhoIsMiniMe" allows its users to seamlessly manage and manipulate their alter egos from one simple phone app. False first impressions are effortlessly minimized with the one-dimensional perfect career avatar called the "Soigne' Self" (French, pronounced swan-yay). The "Soigne' Self" never sees its shadow (and it never lets anyone else see it either) because all users are directed to deposit their secret, private selves into the avatar aptly called the "Shadow Self." And ne'er the two shall meet within the matrix.

Frankly, there appears to be no difference between the strategic actions of a private individual who elects to transfer any detractive character traits off of the public records and onto a self-created "Shadow Self," and the actions of a Lehman Brothers who premeditatedly transfers all of its risky assets off the public books and onto the records of its shady alter ego, Hudson Castle.

Word on the street is that necessity is the mother of invention, and it certainly looks as if the survival of personal privacy in today's voyeuristic climate has necessitated a creative approach to playing the corporate game. So will your virtual, "Soigne' Self," be playing the game to win?

41

Dialing For Your Dollars
June 28, 2010

Being ordinary American consumers, we feel pretty safe in assuming that we're not alone in our diligent commitment to utilizing every possible self-service option at our disposal before we eventually suck it up and make that dreaded 1-800 customer service call for help.

Nothing short of exasperation gone wild can seduce us into thinking that the indefinite phone time on hold (so as to not lose priority placement in the queue, of course) will be worth the wait – a hope briskly shattered the very second a customer service representative answers the line in an unintelligible accent far from home who then launches the dialogue with a monotone recital of some scripted corporate sales pitch, instead of the proper, and expected, "how can I help you?"

They say when one door closes another one opens, yet in the world of guerilla marketing the door seems to simply revolve. Just look **in the rear view mirror** at the national "do not call" registry. Exasperated consumers believed themselves victorious back when the "do not call" list had been legislated for the sole purpose of closing the door on intrusive corporate telemarketers who made it a point to barrage households with unsolicited sales calls at supper time.

But the door never really closed. It just swung around, and now these same telemarketers lay in wait as a captive consumer audience is forced back through the door with an in-coming 1-800 phone call when in need of "customer service" assistance.

There was a time prior to 2010 when a new credit card received in the mail could be easily activated by punching in a few correct numbers from our home phone. Well, it appears those were "the good old days" because now card activating customers are advised to hold on for the service rep whose primary purpose is not to simplify the card activation process, but to promote and sell ancillary add-on products.

Most of the major airline carriers have fairly sophisticated websites filled with important information including policies, security procedures and luggage carry-on restrictions for air travel. When what we needed to know before making a trip abroad couldn't be found on the airline's website, all it took was one phone call ... then another ... and then another, to the airline's 1-800 customer service hot line for us to concede that the phrase "customer service" has now become a front for guerilla corporate marketing.

And as we tried to get an answer to what we thought was an uncomplicated question, we ended up going around the world without ever boarding a plane. First it was Mumbai where she tried to arrange for a rental car without even attempting to answer our question. As she started in on booking a hotel, we hit "Click-End Call." Next it was Jamaica where we were told to go to the website for the answer. "Click-End Call." The last attempt took us to South Africa where he pushed for us to apply for an airline credit card, book a hotel, rent a car. "Click-End Call." After burning up more cell phone time than we care to admit, we were back where we started, answerless.

It's official. The phrase "customer service" has now become another "Oxymoron of the 21st Century," right behind "private sector transparency" and "self-regulation."

The commercials aired on network television aren't what they used to be either. Between the endless election and political smear campaigns trying to buy a vote (maybe we should take a tip from the Brits on this one), and the pharmaceutical commercials looking to medicate the masses, it's all a bunch of white noise that is vapidly fast-forwarded through on the DVR.

As 21st century advertisers persuasively strive to overcome their self-inflicted handicap of marketing to a highly desensitized population, it's painfully obvious that the "Mad Men" days of effective advertising are long gone. The advertising strategies seen today are no longer designed to provide useful or beneficial information, but to assault the senses and provide entertainment; and apparently, with disappointing results.

Most of the country is currently feeling the pinch that squeezes hard during a depressed economy. The call to employ significant cost cutting measures has been heard across the board. Since customer care has evidently depreciated to just about valueless, corporate management has shown it's hardly worth the bother anymore and undeniably merged their sales and marketing departments with "customer service." This little streamlining maneuver goes a long way towards keeping the executive bonus budgets intact.

Every once in a rare while, we gratefully experience the relief that only a true "customer service" professional can administer, and it's as refreshing as a cool mist in the desert. Sick and tired of being sold to, all we really want to know is if there's anyone over at the airlines who can answer our question?

42

Bigger Than Life
September 16, 2010

Our little ITRVM summertime road trip had us thinking that if the Olympic committee were to hand out medals to competing nations based upon how much space they take up, the United States would probably get the Bronze for square footage and the Gold for living large.

Whoever said, "if a little is good, more must be better," succinctly summed up in eight little words humanity's rational propensity towards big and the inherent need to have it all.

One look **in the rear view mirror** at the blueprints for the Tower of Babel reminded us of just how far back this need goes. Unfortunately for Nimrod, the bottom fell out of the biggest-building-in-the-world market when some of his builders showed up for work one day speaking Greek and the jobsite collapsed in chaos.

It hardly seems a coincidence that the big catch phrase for today's Great Depression is "too big to fail." Everything around us is BIG. Too big. And unlike parenthood, no BIG specialist ever got around to publishing some sort of "BIG Manual" to prepare mankind for what going BIG really means, let alone how to keep it going and growing.

Our ignorance to the growing effects of BIG has obviously resulted in an interesting conglomeration of contemporary dilemmas:

Big Food, Big Bodies, Big Medicine

Apparently, the only way our bodies can keep up with the heaping helpings and super-sized meals is to wash everything down with some big gulps and essentially grow bigger all the way around. With the bigger bodies come the bigger health problems, and with the bigger health problems come the bigger medical bills, and with the bigger medical bills come the bigger health insurance premiums, and all of this grows bigger pharmaceutical companies that are fully stocked to medicate the masses for bigger profits.

The old adage, "pay the farmer or pay the doctor," may still hold true when natural and healthy processing standards are adhered to; however, when the farmer becomes so big that it swallows up all of the little farmers, and then fails to protect the health and welfare of the public it's in the business of feeding, we are left with a big country that is largely undernourished.

But there's always room for dessert, and for some that might include bigger breasts, bigger lips, and bigger penises that last longer.

Big Government, Big Deficits, Big Business

It looks as if the turn of the century has delivered unto us a government largely out of balance and deeply mired in the big tasks of war and nation building. Big egos expecting big paybacks proceeded to legislate big spending to bail out their big corporate buddies responsible for mismanaging the industries known as Big Banking, Big Auto, and the Big Boys of Wall Street. This has left the little taxpayers for many generations to come holding a very big bag of debt and a very big tax bill.

Big Housing, Big Transportation, Big Entertainment

There was a time, not so long ago, when Wall Street made it possible for Main Street Americans to live in the McMansion of their dreams with no down payment, thereby blowing the Joneses out of the water. Which was probably doing the Joneses a favor since most of the housing industry is now under water. Not everyone in possession of an underwater mortgage needs to be thrown a life raft though, for some have opted to strategically default on their big mortgages and save money while living free throughout foreclosure until the eviction notice is finally served. Until then, at least they have a nice place to park the big SUV.

Airports have now become so big that they can only be likened to an international sausage factory where every passing second sees thousands of travelers compressed into cat gut casings and tautly squeezed out of the homeland security assembly line like a sausage ready for flight.

The politicians of ancient Rome rarely hesitated to deplete the treasury coffers when it came time to distract the plebian population with really big entertainment. And this time around is certainly no different. We watch our big screens with enormous fascination as big bucks are routinely paid to lure professional athletes and performers with big names to big venues that are oftentimes built in communities where the coffers have been so depleted that city employees have to take pay cuts and the local library is padlocked shut due to lack of funding.

While it didn't take a sea-to-shining-sea road trip to show us that America is filled with a large array of all things BIG, it did show us that the middle isn't the middle anymore. And that TOO BIG is simply too big to manage and a set up for failure.

This made us wonder. How can we possibly declare something "too big to fail" when it's been set up that way?

43

T.S.A.: It's Our Business To Touch Yours
November 21, 2010

The Thanksgiving season has arrived, and with the holiday season comes the opportunity for many of us to slow down long enough to look back **in the rear view mirror** and reminisce with our loved ones about the cornucopian days of old, while giving thanks for barely surviving year 2010 of the Great Depression.

As we watch the price of gas and travel predictably increase in the weeks leading up to every holiday season, we've come to understand that the Wednesday before Thanksgiving is to the travel industry what the Friday after Thanksgiving is to the retail business – namely, the busiest day of the year.

This year is no exception, yet it seems we have last year's underwear bomber to thank for this year's viral travel advisories warning all flyers that airport security has gone "hands-on."

All of the recent brouhaha about passengers being subjected to invasive body searches in exchange for the privilege of boarding a plane with an expensive ticket bought and paid for has us convinced that many travelers will simply explore alternative ways of getting where they want to go with dignity intact.

Considering the hardline screening options flyers have to choose from these days, we can hardly be surprised by the thousands of formal complaints that have already been filed by indignant travelers who believe their rights and bodily temples have been violated.

It doesn't seem to matter whether you choose the Rapiscan radioactive see-you-naked photo op, or opt for the personal touch with a full-body fondling that has been specially designed to intimately search every type of physique – such as "The Gentlemen's Junket" which includes the old "ball and taint lift 'n shift," or the "For Ladies Only" inspection featuring the "camel toe us apart and 'are they real?' breast test."

Whatever screening option you choose (and some lucky passengers may even get to have both), you'll be able to board that airplane with a false sense of security, and of course, the "T.S.A. Approved" inspection stamp conspicuously branded on your hindquarters.

In its arrogance, the T.S.A. has clearly failed in the customer relations department. Perhaps the T.S.A. didn't think it necessary to provide the population that pays for its existence any kind of advanced preparation, let alone a touch of Pavlovian reinforcement through a basic T.S.A. P.S.A. propaganda campaign devised to soothe what they should've anticipated: citizen concerns about rights violations, health risks, and the protection of children who have been taught to never let strangers touch them.

After numerous internet postings went viral, giving viewers access to live and uncensored footage that had been recorded at airport sausage factories across the land by average travelers, potential passengers got to see firsthand what to really expect when they step into a T.S.A. security screening line this holiday season. The T.S.A. has since been forced to play defense and do the damage control dance. It ain't pretty, and it may be their undoing.

Few should be surprised when we begin to see the more customer-oriented, passenger-friendly travel alternatives experience a significant increase in revenue, right about the time the commercial airlines get hit with substantial financial losses once again as they stand on the sidelines and complacently permit the T.S.A. to man-handle their paying passengers, pilots, and flight crews.

The most sickening part of this drama being played out on "security theater" is that everyone knows, even the T.S.A., that the terrorists are way ahead of current policies and procedures. Terrorism has already been found packing its explosive junk all the way up its back trunk where no one can find it without a body cavity search, not even the Rape-i-Scan.

Capitalism may not save us but it does have a tendency to one-up terrorism, for with capitalism comes creative innovation used to create cash flow not martyrs, and just in time for the holiday gift giving season.

There probably isn't one guy on your gift list who wouldn't love hearing this every time he gets a phone call (courtesy of John Tyner), "If you touch my junk, I'm gonna have you arrested!" And if his "junk" is extra special, you might even consider giving your favorite business traveler a pair of radiation briefs with an x-ray blocking fig leaf shield.

Before we know it, those see-you-naked full body scans they say are never stored on a hard drive will be put to good use with the launch of a few trendy websites that'll make celebrity sex videos seem passe'.

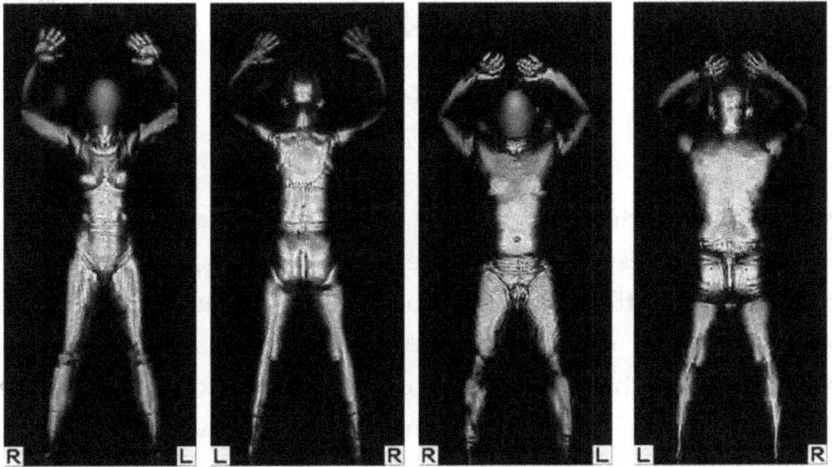

Copyright Disclaimer under Section 107 of the Copyright Act of 1976. Allowance is made for "fair use" for purposes such as commentary, criticism, teaching, education, parody, comedy, research and news reporting.

So it looks like this year will see us celebrating close to home, where we'll be busy giving a special thanks for the fact that we couldn't afford to fly anywhere anyway, even if we were in the mood to get felt up by strangers. Not this year, honey, we have a headache.

44

Walker's Waterloo
March 17, 2011

Something is rotten in the state of Wisconsin, and it's not the moldy bleu cheese. Nor is it the lingering stench of unwashed protestors who filled the Capitol building-turned-campground last month. The rottenness in Wisconsin seems instead to be emanating straight out of the governor's mansion for there's a new man on the throne and he's busy throwing his sceptre around.

In mid-January, Wisconsin's newly elected GOP governor and Tea Party favorite, Scott Walker[1], blindly hit the job post running. Walker wasted no time in outmaneuvering his colleagues before expeditiously stripping his constituents of their collective voice when he ramrodded his "I-owe-the-Koch Brothers" agenda down their throats without so much as a "let's talk about it like grown-ups."

Unreceptive to any form of negotiation, Walker made it clear from the start that he wasn't interested in the opinions of the very people who'd democratically elected him to represent and serve them, even when those voters vehemently jumped up and down in opposition to his rights-stripping legislation. And the fact that Walker's rights-stripping measure had absolutely no bearing on his campaign promises of fiscal responsibility made his imperialistic approach to the issue all the more dehumanizing.

---

[1] **SCOTT WALKER:** Walker was the Republican GOP Governor of Wisconsin from 2011 to 2019 who received motivational campaign funding for "special interests" from the billionaire Koch Brothers.

Apparently, the new face of Tea Party democracy has donned the mask of Napoleon Bonaparte, dictator and self-declared Emperor; and one whom many would assert was the antithesis of democracy.

Maybe Walker simply forgot who was paying him to be their governor, but we hardly think so. As soon as Walker removed his taxpaying population from the equation in one fell swoop of his governor's sceptre, it became quite clear that the man hadn't forgotten who pays him at all – especially when we follow the flow of money along his campaign trail.

Walker has ultimately shown the state of Wisconsin – and the entire nation for that matter – what Harry S. Truman really meant when he said, "the buck stops here." In fact, all indicators are that Walker is vigorously keeping his Tea Party promises of fiscal responsibility even now. Unfortunately for the citizens of Wisconsin, that sense of fiscal responsibility has little to do with them, and everything to do with serving the needs, wants and desires of his financial backers.

To be honest, or not to be honest … … or is that just a stupid question, because Napoleon was of the opinion that "the surest way to remain poor is to be an honest man." And while Napoleon also believed that stupidity wasn't a handicap in politics, everyone knows that no one goes into politics to go poor.

What is most disconcerting about Walker's actions thus far is that no one can really be sure whether his unyielding position is merely the result of a righteous need to champion the cave-man cause of Reaganomics no matter the cost; or if he's been lethally infected with a new strain of the fungus-amungus called the "Koch Bros spores," which would irreversibly turn his empty shell of a body into an American variation of the Zombie Ants of Brazil, and a spore-spreading minion of the Koch Brothers.

A quick glance **in the rear view mirror** at Walker's election campaign contributors shows us just how persuasive a cup of tea steeped in 43,000 spores can be. Evidently the more spores he slurped up, the faster he rose and the stronger he believed himself to be.

Frankly, it would be naïve to think that power didn't come at a price, but with great power also comes great responsibility. Some would call that walking the line, which seems to be a notion very unfamiliar to Walker.

Now that the damage has been done, what we'd like to know is who keeps feeding the fungus-amungus and how is it that the "Koch Bros spores" continue to thrive? Isn't there a way for voters to starve the fungus out?

45

2012 - The Year Of The Job
December 31, 2011

It is often said that things are darkest before the dawn. When we look back **in the rear view mirror** at the passing of 2011, we find little solace in the fact that we were not alone when it came to navigating the stressful demands of a great depression and the transformative social unrest it has given rise to.

The plight of struggling Americans all across the country this year gone by has been disheartening. And their plight has, for the most part, been shamefully minimized as elected officials from every constituency continue to dismiss the public demonstrations of their voting population.

Nor have any of the people's protests prevented our legislative representatives from secretly re-routing our resources away from the very infrastructure that is necessary to improve the livelihoods for those who embody the backbone of America.

Instead, the preferential beneficiary of these resources appears to be the "new people" – a "new people" furtively created by the Supreme Court under its "Citizens United" ruling, and comprised of the well-endowed institutions known collectively as Corporate America.

Every living and breathing human has a right to contribute and take up space, and it's time we occupy our space with confidence.

Power to the real people! Stand up and be noticed in 2012 because everyone knows it's the squeaky wheel that gets the grease.

46

The New GOP – Gender Overlord Party
March 5, 2012

Nothing breeds the need to manipulate the masses faster than an election year. And those who are financially serious about securing their prominent positions of power never abort their efforts to win, even in the between times.

This means there can be no safety net or escape for the targeted masses being manipulated. Wherever they turn, they are being routinely subjected to an onslaught of emotional torture that we can only liken to waterboarding because every assault has been psychologically programmed to wear them down and negatively feed into their deepest fears. At this point, one might even suggest that the masses have been morally imprisoned by the propaganda that has been unmercifully pouring down upon them without reprieve for more than a few decades and then some.

And when we try to unearth whose moral standards are calling the shots these days, we find ourselves standing in very murky waters with old world sludge oozing through our toes.

The United States of America, Inc. has proudly boasted for generations a constitutional foundation that supports equality and religious freedom for all of its national citizenry. These very liberties are part of what makes America a desirable place to live not only for those who live here, but for many around the world; yet, the last decade has seen a disturbing trend that seems to be intent upon eroding these individual and very personal rights.

A recent case in point would be the Supreme Court's "Citizens United" decision two years ago. This abominable judicial decision was a huge 100-year leap back in time for the living and breathing humans of this nation, and a testimony to the tenacity of corporate greed. Today's presidential election, and the Super PACs secretly funding it, are real time proof to anyone who mistakenly thought things would be different a century later that history will always repeat itself when given the chance.

Another case in point brings us to the current race to win the 2012 GOP presidential nomination. The inflammatory, yet bizarrely virtuous, campaign rhetoric being hurled from every conservative pulpit and right-right newsroom this election season has evidently chosen to unilaterally hone in on publicly debating what should constitute morally appropriate healthcare for the female population as if it was a vital political issue.

It's no secret that the push to repeal the healthcare reform legislation of 2010 has been a primary objective for the GOP from the beginning. Yet, for reasons righteously hidden behind a veil of morality, the bulk of the conservative argument has suspiciously winged to the far right to hover around limiting healthcare coverage for women. And this has all been done without ever mentioning, let alone giving equal measure to the discussion of, what limitations ought to likewise be placed upon the healthcare coverage for the male population.

Many spiritual enthusiasts are quick to espouse the holy notion that every body is a temple, which today would translate to mean that approximately 309 million American temples are in need of medical maintenance at any given point in time, and some will need more maintenance than others. At around 157 million, more than half of these bodily temples are female in gender.

This makes the disturbing fact that not one female was allowed to speak on behalf of the nation's women on February 16, 2012 when

House Oversight Committee Chairman, Darrell Issa (R-CA), called together an all male panel to discuss the moral prudence of covering contraception for women as an allowable component of affordable healthcare all the more alarming.

So when did an exclusionary panel of Moby Dicks[1] become the morality overlords for a nation?

When we consider the old world inspiration for our current civilization and the Latin-based language we speak, the best answer to that question today will likely be found by looking back **in the rear view mirror** at ancient Rome.

To say that ancient Rome was a patriarchal society, and a world power once committed to conquering the entire known world including the Eurasian continent without compunction, would be an understatement. As unbelievable as it may seem in our so called "modern world," only adult free men could be called citizens of ancient Rome. Patrician lineage notwithstanding, Roman women were never granted citizenship, nor were they given legal rights, because Roman men believed that a woman was unable to direct her own activities and must therefore be kept under male guardianship at all times. Women were bargaining chips for their fathers and brothers to use in negotiating marriage alliances, and they were expected to be subservient and obedient to their husbands in all things.

---

[1] **MOBY DICK** (Archetype): A **male** "MOWB" and a name sometimes used to refer to Ex-VP Dick Cheney. **MOLDY OLD WHITE BREAD, or "MOWB"** (Archetype): A tasty depiction of a human anachronism who routinely derives sustenance from stale, inedible, and moldy ways of thinking, while advocating modus operandi that is firmly entrenched in standards set by the "Old Guard." MOWBs are not conservatively categorized or necessarily stereotyped by gender, age, race, culture, or even political party affiliation; but usually reveal their unmistakable MOWB-ness with a mindset deeply rooted in entitlement, arrogance, superiority and double standards.

For all intents and purposes, Roman women were chattel. They had no open voice in society, they could not vote, and they could not make decisions about what was best for their own bodies. And this included birthing babies. If a Roman woman did not produce the children required of her by a guardian husband, she could be divorced and abandoned with barely a word.

Conquering the known world required brute force. Something the Romans were pretty good at. But the subtle art of successfully subduing those civilizations once conquered required a more integrative touch. And history reveals that the Romans were pretty good at that too. They were not above placating the conquered by co-mingling spiritual belief systems just enough to create an umbrella of religious unification which provided a little something for everyone.

Regardless of the tenets outlined within "original scripture," this practice continued to thrive throughout the doctrinal evolution of the Roman Catholic Church from its inception in the 4th century C.E. The practice was permanently discontinued when religious tolerance by the Church was no longer necessary to unify the masses because its powerful political position in the conquered known world had been firmly secured during the Inquisition. A few centuries of fear and torture, and behold! Upon this platform stands the history of a Roman Catholic Church that managed to brutally seize control, formalize its omnipotence, and of course, solidify its right to call the self-serving shots.

So when we fast forward two thousand years and find ourselves struggling to get by on a right wing and a prayer, we find it impossible to overlook the obvious as we watch the re-enactment of old Roman ideologies playing themselves out in the form of Roman Catholic Church standard operating procedures on our "modern day" Congressional floor. 2008 GOP presidential candidate, Mike Huckabee, could not have said it better when he recently declared on behalf of the GOP, "We are all Catholics now!"

This sweeping pronouncement has given us a new meaning for the Grand Old Party's "GOP" acronym. In full recognition of our bullying times, we believe a more fitting definition for the new GOP[1] would be the "Gender Overlord Party." And it appears so far that the new GOP will have no trouble living up to this new definition, particularly when it comes to lording it over the people with righteousness and dogma.

Calling the principled shots for the masses can be a polarizing proposition, especially when the new GOP has chosen to mimic the double-standard-setting leadership of a Catholic Church that is supremely un-inclined to even follow its own Biblical rulebook. The eroding effects of this bipolar platform are difficult to avoid given the endless barrage of mass-manipulating mixed messages that border on schizophrenic being showered upon the nation. For in its self-appointed role of morality police, the new GOP has waterboarded the masses mercilessly with the "Who, What, Where, When, and How" of things that should be done in order to conform within a limiting definition of what constitutes a God-fearing America: WHO to do it with, WHAT to do, WHERE to do it, WHEN to do it, and HOW to do it.

All equal consideration aside, we suppose in the end, acquiring the power necessary to call the self-serving shots has always come

---

[1] **GOP: GENDER OVERLORD PARTY**, or "The New GOP" for short (A Cultural Mindset): The "GOP" acronym known for centuries in the United States to stand for the Republican "Grand Old Party" has been updated to be the new signifier for the "Gender Overlord Party." This turn of the 21st century revision was made in order to better reflect the bullying nature and evolving cultural mindset of a GOP that has elected to stand on a platform righteously rooted in conflict, contradiction and condescension.

down to the money, because he who controls the money gets to make the rules. Whether the mass manipulation is effectuated through the fear of hellfire and damnation or the fear of financial failure and ruin, it really doesn't seem to matter. The powerful end-results for those seeking to call the shots are all the same.

As the new GOP myopically strives to reprise the glory days of ancient Rome in 21st century America, they might want to take a hard look at the Arab Spring and consider what the masses are capable of when they have had enough of the Old Guard man-handling.

As for the American masses being man-handled, this time in history appears to be a pivotal time of choice for the population of a great nation. We can choose to step back in time and surrender our power to those seeking to grab it away through intimidation, or we can choose to step up to the plate and make a stand for the kind of collective society we truly want to have. To choose nothing would be to surrender to the power grab. And should enough of us choose to go down that illusionary road of safe surrender, we will ultimately have little option but to put an aspirin between our legs and blame Rome for all our troubles.

So fellow Americans, it looks like we are in this together whether we choose to be or not. What kind of collective society do you believe is worth voting and standing up for?

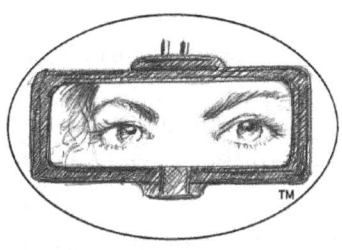

ITRVM Dream Sequences

DREAM SEQUENCE:
An ITRVM Allegory where we weave things together that don't seem to go together to create a vision of things to come. We liken these to random, off-road detours along the lookout ledge of our own private Idaho. We also like to call these "Crazy Ivans."

47

Camp Fed Takes The Triple
Dream Sequence, February 2, 2009

We had a dream ... and in that dream we observed a small herd of wild deer grazing on the dewy morning grasses of Morgantown's "Camp Fed" minimum security prison peacefully located amid West Virginia's rolling Blue Ridge Mountains. The deer startled and quickly fled as a hotel-type shuttle van approached the compound with its latest inductees.

It was difficult to identify the three newbies as they emerged from the shuttle van looking like a fraternity trifecta in matching cardigan sweaters because the bright morning sun caused them to instinctively block their faces with arms and hands against the glare. When they turned to enter the facility, we could then see Camp Fed's three new inmates were I-ROB[1], BERNIE[2], and BLAGO[3].

---

[1] **I-ROB**: John A. Thain, former CEO of Merrill Lynch who resigned on January 22, 2009, right before Bank of America CEO Ken Lewis could sack him. Mr. Fix-It proposed the shotgun wedding between Merrill and BofA and their CEOs, which abruptly ended in annulment barely 3 months later (didn't something like that happen with Rene' Zellweger and Kenny Chesney?). BofA gobbled up Merrill's enormous deficit and naturally passed the tab on to the taxpayers in the form of TARP bailout funding. I-ROB smoothly managed to expend $1.22 Million to make his office feel more like home, and to secretly disburse $4 Billion in early employee bonuses before dashing off to Vail, Colorado for a year-end ski holiday just as Merrill's $15.3 Billion 2008 4Q loss was announced. AKA "I-ROBOT" for his mechanical coldness, void of emotion and intense financial focus.

[2] **BERNIE**: Bernard L. Madoff. Chairman and Founder of Bernard L. Madoff Investment Securities LLC, 1960. Arrested on December 11, 2008 and sentenced to 150 years of quiet meditation, Bernie currently (as of 2009) awaits his formal induction into the Ponzi Hall of Fame. AKA: the Jewish Treasury Bill and the new face of Greed. He was formerly a philanthropist, a regular family man about town, and a prominent leader in the financial services industry who gave

Our dream flowed on as the threesome processed through formal registration, got secured with new electronic monitoring ankle bracelets, and exchanged their cardigans for the prison's standard issue khaki uniforms. Their next stop was the media room for inmate orientation.

The privileged trio were shown a specially prepared 15-minute video starring Martha Stewart on how to make the most of their lives on the inside. She reminded them that while Camp Fed may be no Camp Cupcake, it was still a Camp No Dough. They would have to earn their 12 to 40 cents/hour working a full 7-1/2 hour day. Martha further encouraged them by quoting the famous words of Nelson Mandela who said, "many, many good people have gone to prison." The video concluded with Martha's dangled promise to personally host a catered "if you aren't indicted, you aren't invited" party at her Westchester County estate upon their release.

We were surprised by how well the trinity adjusted to their new lifestyles.

I-ROB found the Lord and was saved. He renounced his materialistic ways and took a solemn vow of poverty. His intensity was now focused toward brokering the best deal he could with the Almighty in his new position as prison Savior of

---

everyone he was screwing the big KISS (keep it simple, stupid) of financial, and sometimes literal, death.

[3] **BLAGO**: Milorad "Rod" R. Blagojevich. He was a record holder as the first Illinois governor to ever be impeached on January 29, 2009. He made sure to jet back to his Chicago home before the Senate's final vote could formalize his civilian status and deprive him of the ride home from Springfield on the state plane. Blago notoriously tried to sell The Big BOPR's (aka Barack Obama) vacated senate seat to the highest bidder and had the misfortune of being wiretapped along the way. While he insisted he was the victim of a rush to judgment, it kinda looks like he did a Nixon and just got caught doing what everyone else has always done. It's all gonna be bleepin' golden in jail.

Souls (SOS) liaison. Interesting though, even with all that, there was still no forthcoming mea culpa.

BERNIE was thrilled to see his dorm room required no redecorating. Things were in perfect balance with black drab, sterile white and shades of gray. He spent his 7-1/2 hour work days teaching the other inmates how they too could build a pyramid that would put Giza to shame. It's all about the "KISS."

BLAGO spent his working days calling every publisher he could find with a toll free number looking to sell his story to the highest bidder. He just knew his biography, "One Day a Peacock, the Next Day a Feather Duster," would reveal the true man behind the myth. When Blago wasn't pimping his book, he was busy negotiating with the "Morgantown Madam" to get a covert call girl operation off the ground because, well, he knew people who'd pay and wasn't about to let that go to waste. It's important to take full advantage of every opportunity while it's hot. Some would call that making lemonade out of lemons.

And then we woke up wondering if three really was a crowd. Or was it more of a triangular way to cover their backsides, which we suspect came in handy when one of them had the misfortune of dropping his bar of soap in the showers?

48

The Devil's In The Details
Dream Sequence, March 16, 2009

We had a dream ... and in that dream we saw Bernie[1] stretched out on his bunk after suiting up in the standard issue baggy brown uniform of his new Metropolitan Correctional Center home. His arms were folded beneath his head as he stared blankly at the empty mattress resting on the bunk above him, barely two feet from his face. He was waiting for the cell doors to release for the Center's pre-dawn breakfast call, and the start of a new day on the inside.

Unquestionably, Bernie's current situation was a far cry indeed from the $7 Million Upper East Side penthouse apartment he'd been accustomed to. Lifestyle adjustments needed to be made, especially since his new home work detail assigned him to Biffy Patrol.

In our dream we could see confusion ripple across Bernie's face when the prison Custodial Super slapped a large rolling mop bucket and toilet brush into his hands. Without expression, Bernie walked into the janitor's closet to collect whatever else he thought he might need to properly clean something he'd never cleaned before in his life.

---

[1] **BERNIE**: Bernard L. Madoff, Chairman and Founder of Bernard L. Madoff Investment Securities LLC, 1960. Arrested on December 11, 2008 and sentenced to 150 years of quiet meditation, Bernie currently (as of 2009) awaits his formal induction into the Ponzi Hall of Fame. AKA: the Jewish Treasury Bill and the new face of Greed. He was formerly a philanthropist, a regular family man about town, and a prominent leader in the financial services industry who gave everyone he was screwing the big KISS (keep it simple, stupid) of financial, and sometimes literal, death.

Bernie was clearly ignorant to the world of cleaning products and before anyone would even suspect what he was unwittingly capable of that day in the janitor's closet, he'd whipped up a chlorine bleach-ammonia cleaning concoction which rapidly created a noxious gas that overpowered and expeditiously knocked him to the floor, thus ending his life here on Earth.

Bernie briefly lay unconscious before the ethereal lights began to flicker as his life force separated from the 70-year old body with finality. Out of nowhere appeared Charles Ponzi, Bernie's personal escort and Angel of Death, with outstretched hand.

Ponzi ushered Bernie through a misty elevator door and pressed the button going "down." Bernie would now be answering to a new overlord, the Prince of Darkness, in a personal hell of his own creation. Mr. D (as the Prince liked to be called) had a friendly chat with Bernie as they walked down a deep corridor lined with doors on both sides. Every door they passed was numbered "666."

When Mr. D finally stopped at the door numbered "666" belonging to Bernie, he opened it and extended his arm in a welcoming gesture of entry. Bernie's mind swirled with déjà vu' as he found himself walking right back into the very 7-1/2' x 8' janitor's closet his body had just died in. His new work detail would keep him busy for an eternity, for he was to count out $65 Billion dollars, one penny at a time.

And then we woke up and realized that the I.R.S. has collected tax revenue for decades from Bernie's investor clients based upon illusionary gains reported for investments they never even had. We suspect hell will need to freeze over before the I.R.S. gives any of that revenue back.

But what we really want to know is which one of Bernie's little helpers will be the next to follow his lead?

49

When Karma Comes Calling
Dream Sequence, April 5, 2009

We had a dream ... and in that dream we saw The Hague's International Criminal Court receive a formally filed complaint, with no return address, from Osama Bin Laden against former U.S. President, George W. Bush, and his ex-partner former VP, Dick Cheney, for crimes against humanity, war of aggression, and war crimes.

Through the haze we observed The Hague's ICC judiciary committee collectively scoff at Osama's audacity in filing such a complaint. In their minds, it all boiled down to the pot calling the kettle black, and there was absolutely no reason for the international courts to get all snarled up in any he-said-he-said finger pointing between a couple of has-beens.

With a snap, snap, and two rolls of the wrist, Bin Laden fully expected enthusiastic obeisance and immediate compliance to his cave issued directives, and The Hague's dismissive response to his perfectly legitimate complaint proved unacceptable. Our dream rolled along as Bin Laden proceeded to mastermind a black op campaign in true jihadic fashion against his two war-on-terror antagonists.

No detail was left to chance and limitless financing oiled the way. Osama knew the well-trained and cash-strapped Blackwater-now-Xe[1] mercenaries were a perfect fit for his rendition mission code named "Pay Back's a Bitch."

---

[1] **BLACKWATER**: Blackwater Worldwide was an American military contractor (mercenary army) founded by Erik Prince who was a Navy SEAL and CIA asset. It was reputed to be VP Dick Cheney's mercenary army of choice during the

Xe's top secret mercenaries covertly commandeered two scrapped RAH-66 Comanche stealth helicopters with flawless precision. Like ninjas, the mercenary crews were dressed in black from head to toe, including full facemask coverage, as each chopper mobilized to pick up its respective cargo before coming together at 0300 hours below the radar in Nevada's well-guarded Area 51 where the Jeppesen jet was standing by.

Chopper 1's southern target was the Preston Hollow burb of Dallas to snatch up XP "W[1]," while Chopper 2 veered north to seize Cheney from his Wyoming ranch.

The Dallas crew had to silently tread undetected through dozens of scattered empty Bud Lite cans before ultimately finding XP "W" sprawled and snoring on his game room couch, mouth agape and spittle drying into its crusty corners. Barney the dog barely stirred from his curled sleeping position on the floor to glance nonchalantly at the swarming ninjas.

Cheney was discovered in his ranch house dozing on a therapeutic bed in the guest room because apparently it was better for his back. On the nightstand beside him was a heavily dog-eared copy of Orwell's "Animal Farm" resting in opened, face down position next to a dimly lit pig-shaped lamp capped with a swinish caricature of Cheney's face in full snout.

On a screen split between 1,400 miles, we continued to watch as the two abduction crews synchronistically blindfolded, bound and gagged their captives, cut off their clothes, administered each

---

Bush Administration from 2001 to 2008. Blackwater changed its name to Xe in 2009.

[1] **XP "W"**: Ex-President George W. Bush, 43rd President of the United States of America, Inc., officially sworn in to office January 20, 2001. He served two disastrous 4-year terms then finally crashed and burned his way out on January 19, 2009. He was succeeded by The Big BOPR (aka Barack Obama).

an enema and powerful sleeping drugs, outfitted them in diapers then finally jumpsuits – all critical steps specifically designed to prepare the kidnapped ex's for a very long rendition flight to black stop destination number one in Turkey.

As Cheney was tossed aboard the Jeppesen alongside an incoherent and moaning XP "W," he recoiled even through heavy sedation when he recognized the surrounding voices of their captors as those belonging to his former "VP-only" super-secret death squad. Ex-VP Cheney dully realized before losing all consciousness that any pledge of allegiance once given to him by this group of clandestine professionals was forsaken the very moment he stopped paying them.

The rendition rollercoaster ride zigzagged unpredictably for weeks, months, years from one black site hideaway to another - from Turkey to North Korea, then Iran, Iraq, Somalia, eventually winding down in the recently-vacated Guantanamo Bay. And there were plenty of waterboard confessionals to go around.

Bin Laden required every waterboard interrogation to be videotaped and was dumbfounded as XP "W" and Cheney consistently blamed each other for all accused wrongdoing, under the compulsively steadfast belief that they were themselves true innocents, without culpability.

Blame shifting video montages full of "It was his fault, not mine!" and "He did it, not me!" were released to the only true news media outlets left in America that Osama Bin Laden trusted to deliver the story straight up: Jon Stewart and Stephen Colbert. He'd had second thoughts about asking for a ransom because he didn't think anyone would pay it and frankly, he didn't really need the money.

And then we woke up and realized the Universe has a sense of justice all its own, with a sense of humor to match. So will Jon Stewart and Stephen Colbert make us laugh or leave us quivering in our boots when they deliver the latest breaking news of XP "W" and Cheney's comeuppance delivered at the hands of their greatest nemesis and Public Enemy #1?

50

The Salon Beyond
Dream Sequence, July 11, 2009

We had a dream ... and in that dream we found ourselves ascending so swiftly that the Milky Way vanished in the blink of an eye as we made our way ever higher into the Great Beyond.

Moving with such great speed, we never expected the abrupt halt and free fall that deposited us directly in the middle of a grand opening celebration apparently in full swing. Regrettably, we'd missed the silver cord cutting ceremony only two weeks earlier.

Above us flew a myriad of banners that were being pulled behind winged astral bodies like something seen at the beach in the summertime when those little airplanes fly along the coastline with banner advertisements for captive viewing sunbathers. These Great Beyond banners all read, "CHANGE YOUR HAIR, CHANGE YOUR NEXT LIFE."

By the looks of it, Farrah Fawcett's new hair salon was the mane event. Personalities were lined up around Orion's Belt waiting for the rare opportunity to co-create either a do-over or a make-over of their next incarnation, and Farrah's guarantee was hair to define you.

Some recent additions to the ethers patiently waited in line for their turn in the stylist's chair. We smiled as they peacefully submitted to Farrah's angelic touch, and the vision of another walk around the wheel of life. One by one they came, and we listened as they ordered up their next experience:

Robert McNamara[1] was poised to receive the full complement of serving his country, and promptly requisitioned a Jarhead Buzz cut to go along with his new hard body for a lifetime of service on the front lines.

Ed McMahon decided he had absolutely no intention of going out broke the next time around and immediately ordered up "The Donald" Cotton Candy Comb Over.

Michael Jackson quickly grabbed his crotch before floating in backwards toward the chair in a moon walk. He knew for a fact that growing up sucks and requested the life of a little person with Shirley Temple ringlets.

Karl Malden got an ego boost with a sculptured nose job by Michelangelo, which fit nicely with his newly styled Mullet, because now it was all business in the front and party in the back. The Davidesque nose + Mullet cut combo, augmented with a flaming farmer's tan and new GM pickup, would make him a babe magnet for sure.

Mr. Infomercial Billy Mays insisted on getting volumized with Blago[2] Hair products not only because "It's Bleep'n Golden," but

---

[1] **ROBERT STRANGE McNAMARA**: McNamara was the longest serving U.S. Secretary of Defense from 1961 to 1968 under the administrations of John F. Kennedy and Lyndon B. Johnson. He played a major role in promoting U.S. involvement in Vietnam. Upon resigning his post as Secretary of Defense, he became president of the World Bank from 1968 to 1981.

[2] **BLAGO**: Milorad "Rod" R. Blagojevich. He was a record holder as the first Illinois governor to ever be impeached on January 29, 2009. He made sure to jet back to his Chicago home before the Senate's final vote could formalize his civilian status and deprive him of the ride home from Springfield on the state plane. Blago notoriously tried to sell The Big BOPR's (aka Barack Obama) vacated senate seat to the highest bidder and had the misfortune of being wiretapped along the way. While he insisted he was the victim of a rush to judgment, it kinda looks like he did a Nixon and just got caught doing what everyone else has always done. It's all gonna be bleepin' golden in jail.

because he knew that if he could sell Oxi-Clean and Kaboom, he could sell a seat in the Senate without getting busted.

And then we woke up and wondered if the philosophy "as above, so below" holds true, then wouldn't "CHANGE YOUR HAIR, CHANGE YOUR LIFE" work for us right now?

51

Ticker Trade
Dream Sequence, August 7, 2009

We had a dream ... and in that dream we found ourselves hidden in the shadows near a second level banister that offered an unobstructed view of the active trading floor below and a panoramic ticker tape above. The open outcries reverberating from down in the pit were jumbled and chaotic, yet clearly influenced the ticker symbols as they scrolled along without delay.

First glance led us to believe we were observing a typical work day at the New York Mercantile Exchange (NYMEX), but something was amiss. The surprising sight of rabbi traders peppered throughout the pit seemed highly unusual.

It was then we noticed the large gold-plated letters affixed to the wall above the trading room floor which read: RED SHIELD ORGAN TRANSPLANT EXCHANGE (ROTEX). The signage was positioned underneath an emblematic logo displaying an inverted golden medical Caduceus centered on an ornate Red Shield[1].

We inaudibly gasped upon realizing we were really somewhere in New Jersey watching an unsanctioned commodities market trade in body parts on the world market.

As the symbols continued their repetitious flow across the ticker, we began to piece the parts together and the first piece belonged to black market capitalism. Heartless profiteering resounded throughout the pit below as kidneys, livers, pancreases, hearts,

---

[1] **RED SHIELD**: The Rothschild Banking Family.

lungs, eyes, appendages, bones, skin grafts, and even soft tissues were being traded, hedged, arbitraged, forwarded, and futured for obscene under-the-surgical-table profits.

Our dream ticked along as many of the dark secrets surrounding ROTEX and its membership roster were unmasked. Member traders had been covertly cultivated and sponsored by the guts and bowels of health insurance heavyweights, and admittance didn't come cheap. Although membership proved to be extremely expensive, cost was secondary to the covenant of absolute secrecy, and all members were blood-bound for life to a "Skull and Bones" code of silence.

The rise of ROTEX had naturally spawned the unquestionable need for a highly sophisticated organ matchmaker rating system similar to that of other legitimate commodities markets, and the "Serpent Index" was unrivaled in its ability to grade donor quality, provide organ inventory stats and harvest projections, and rate body part pools for securitizing.

And then we woke up and understood that when it comes down to the business of selling a person's body parts, society's moral line seems to be drawn at "if it can't grow back, it can't be sold." However, the indisputable human instinct for survival can sadly provoke those facing serious financial challenges to cross that moral line when desperation dominates, even if it means survival minus a part.

But what we really want to know is did those organ brokers first cut out and trade in their own hearts before turning to profit on the illicit innards of human beings in dire straits?

52

Reinczarnation
Dream Sequence, September 11, 2009

We had a dream ... and in that dream we saw Nicholas II, the last Czar of Imperial Russia, standing with great distinction in his trademark uniform before an otherworldly horde of dearly departed leaders from history past.

The people's revolution was as much a thing of the past as the eclectic group standing before him, but after Czar Nicholas had been officially canonized "Saint Nicholas the Passion-Bearer," his ethereal vocation aspired to that of magisterial guardian.

History's penchant for repetition supported Saint Nick's dreamy notion that there was no time better than the present to decree the reincarnation of a new Czar-based administration consisting of several well-chosen individual Czars, each to be placed in charge of its own single-purpose fiefdom.

Consideration for each incarnated inauguration was to be based solely upon the candidate's special abilities, and not necessarily upon any aptitude for running an empire. Saint Nick immersed himself accordingly into the rigid Czar selection process by meticulously profiling this pool of old world ringleaders and how their best abilities could be utilized.

Although Nicky had plenty of royal relatives to pick from, our dream showed that he had no propensity toward nepotism this time around, for his elevated position had offered him an awareness level enhanced enough to realize that ancestry does not always a good Czar make.

And so we watched as he threw himself into the momentous task of divvying up his old Czar job between some of the local talent:

BANK CZAR: **J. P. Morgan**. Don't just control it, own it all.

BIG TOBACCO TAR CZAR: **Sitting Bull** and **Crazy Horse**, Co-Czars. Teepees, hookahs, and riding the "Wild West" war path going East.

CAR CZAR: **Genghis Khan**. An all-terrain Land Rover with the ability to conquer invaded markets.

CENSUS CZAR: **Pol Pot**. Committed to keeping the numbers manageable.

CYBER CZAR: **J. Edgar Hoover**. Where paranoia is the name of the game.

DOCTRINE CZAR: **Torquemada** and **Saladin**, Co-Czars. A perfect blend of "it's the one true religion or the rack" and jihadic crusadism.

DRUG CZAR: **Ronald Reagan**. Just say NO.

FOOD CZAR: **Henry VIII**. Corpulence is King!

HEALTH CZAR: **Achilles**. An uncompromising mercenary with a talent for strategy and group motivation, in spite of that little hitch in his giddy-up. Second runner up for the post was Empress Alexandra's favorite, **RasPUTIN**.

INSURANCE CZAR: **Il Duce, Benito Mussolini**. Fascism meets survival of the fittest.

PAY CZAR: **Julius Caesar**. Rape, pillage, and enforcement of the "if you scratch my back, I'll scratch your back" bonus payment system.

TARP[1] CZAR: **John D. Rockefeller**. Failure is not an option, especially when you're big.

And then we woke up and realized that by assigning these historical vanguards a mini-Czardom in accordance with their best abilities, Nicholas had unwittingly employed a basic tenet of the very ideology that had ultimately rendered him impotent and superfluous. While communist credo had promised the people, "From each according to his ability, to each according to his need," the overall consensus seems to be that the people never really did get what they needed, regardless of the regime ruling the land.

It appears the real Czars assigned to do the regulatory paperwork these days, however, are merely public relations puppets whose strings are being adroitly manipulated by some unseen puppet master hidden behind a stage curtain. Will this Grand Puppet Master ever come out into the light and offer us unveiled illumination?

---

[1] **TARP** (Troubled Asset Relief Program) is a direct result of the Emergency Economic Stabilization Act of October, 2008 (aka "Bank Bailout of 2008" and "Wall Street Bailout") enacted by President George W. Bush which allowed the U.S. government to use taxpayer funds to the tune of $700 Billion to purchase toxic assets and equity from failing banks/financial institutions in order to prop up and prevent a total financial sector collapse said to be due in part to the subprime mortgage crisis.

53

Rise Of The Global Republic
Dream Sequence, September 27, 2009

We had a dream ... and in that dream we saw Julius Caesar riding into Pittsburgh for the G-20 Summit on his white horse, just about the time Libya's Colonel Gaddafi was trying to pitch his party tent on The Donald's Bedford lawn. It took 94 minutes for Caesar to maneuver through the fray of plebeian protesters before triumphantly marching up the civic center steps where the new millennium's world leaders were assembled en masse under the banner of economy and democracy.

Caesar may have lost a battle or two in his day, but he never lost a war, and his dark-age old debate with Jupiter was no different. None of the gods were surprised to see Jupiter finally acquiesce in allowing Gaius Julius to transcend the millennial span on a dream ride into 2009 A.D. so he could see what remained of his illustrious Roman legacy.

Sitting astride his fine steed, Toes, in the middle of Pittsburgh, Caesar broadly surveyed his modern day surroundings, took inventory of what old Republic hand-me-downs were still in evidence today, and made a summary assessment of Roman contribution to 21st century operations.

Every direction he surveyed prominently flaunted vestiges of ancient Roman-Greco urban master planning. J.C. found himself surrounded by a forum of modern day government buildings, civic centers offering public gathering places, plenty of holy temples to the gods, sports stadiums modeled after the beloved Coliseum, amphitheatres for the performing arts, parks, and even the standard victory parade route.

Togas were obviously out, and sadly there was not a public bath house in sight. The closest he could get was a 24-Hour Fitness and everyone he saw sweating in the window had their clothes on ... well, sort of. Surprised by the overall plumpness of the populous not sweating at the gym, Caesar thought a vomitorium comeback might not be such a bad idea.

And the month of July? It was still coming around once a year right in time for his birthday.

While he can't take credit for the Caesar Salad or the lifesaving Caesarean Section (even though he and Queen Cleo did have a son named Caesarion), J.C. was shocked to see that his melting pot blend-n-merge approach to religious doctrinal unification had been cast aside in favor of pronounced civil dissention born out of intolerance and arrogant sect supremacy.

Back in Caesar's prime time, marriages were simply mergers designed to create corporate-styled alliances for the purpose of growing the family business. He could see little had changed in that arena. As far as strong, powerful women who knew how to rule a kingdom went, few could equal Cleopatra in his experience (and his cousin and old buddy Marc Antony could back him up on that one). As far as women knowing their place in a man's world, it looked as if the campaign for gender equality was still waging on.

Little seems to have changed in the political arena as well. He watched as those G-20 global governments predictably finessed their way through the agenda in the traditional part-democratic, part-oligarchic elitist manner he knew so well. Caesar did, however, find the new Republic's budgetary crisis a bit intriguing. Perhaps that's because Rome had ruled for a millennium without ever having a budget. He couldn't help but laugh though when he heard the familiar high-pitched squeals of the upper classes when the subject of them paying taxes came up, again. Some things just never change.

Gaius Julius Caesar had naturally been born into patrician high society, yet he'd always prided himself on being a populist and man of the people. The Republic of Rome was more important than the individuals it was comprised of, and he was pleased to hear that a contemporary world leader named John F. Kennedy had kept the torch burning when he proclaimed, "ask not what your country can do for you, ask what you can do for your country."

After gloriously expanding Rome's real estate holdings during the course of an exemplary military career, Caesar could deservedly declare in triumph, "I came, I saw, I conquered." Unfortunately, the fateful demise of Julius Caesar didn't occur on the battlefield as one would expect, but it came shrouded in cowardice from those closest to him. Like the Roman Republic itself, Caesar was taken out from within. Et tu, Brute'?

And then we woke up and knew the die had been cast. It seems the world leader crusaders have mobilized a campaign in earnest to defend democracy as the new religion, and internationalism as the new book of doctrine. As the crusaders press on for absolute global conversion, do we need to worry that the new global government will become too big to fail?

54

Casanova Works The Strip
Dream Sequence, October 17, 2009

We had a dream … and in that dream we found ourselves observing the high stakes action at a back room baccarat table in The Venetian Hotel, Las Vegas. The croupier was plumed to perfection as an 18th century Italian dandy – replete with the requisite powdered pony periwig – and the plastic name tag pinned to his left lapel was engraved with the name: CASANOVA - VENICE, ITALY.

A fresh deck of cards had been shuffled and cut, and the distinguished high rollers partaking in this very exclusive game of tomcat baccarat deliberately placed their ample bets on the table. Without delay, Casanova smoothly put the game in to play as he pitched the cards with precision to the roundtable of punting philanderers sitting before him.

Money was clearly no object to the big spending playboys who'd paid dearly for the privilege of being in the presence of the master of amore' in the fleeting hopes that the master might throw a few lessons in the art of seduction their way, mano a mano. They gazed upon Casanova with veneration, and like puppies in love, waited with bated breath for him to bestow his tutelage upon them.

Our dream had cleverly dealt us an unexpected fusion of old world sagacity with new world emulation.

Being an observant man, Casanova felt it prudent to properly assess the skill level of the libertines seeking his instruction before doling out any sort of enlightenment. The swingers that were now gaping at him admiringly were overall a lamentable and disappointing array of wannabes, and he felt almost as if he'd be offering the precious gift of manhood to amateurs.

While Casanova knew nothing about men being from Mars or women coming from Venus, he did know that if any of these lotharios had bothered to read his memoirs, they would've saved themselves, not only a lot of money given the high price of his game, but loads of humiliation as well.

Casanova decided to begin their initiation with the basics, namely, his "ImaRAKE" technique because the condensed wisdom he'd managed to distill from his life's work would provide a succinct summarization of what was required to perpetuate the art of managing a successful seduction.

"ImaRAKE" in four easy steps:

Step 1.	**R**ESCUE said damsel in distress from her current oppressive lover or unpleasant situation.
Step 2.	**A**LLEVIATE said damsel's distress, console, comfort, and champion her.
Step 3.	**K**ISS her seductively, and move on to passionate consummation.
Step 4.	**E**XIT STRATEGY, which should always include the popular, "I'm not worthy," and, "You deserve better," for a friendly, yet conclusive parting of the ways.

Of course, had they all practiced his tried and true "Ima**RAKE**" in four easy steps, they'd still be shamelessly cavorting with an inspirational Muse with Benefits[1] today.

Upon stressing to his ardent pupils that no man is the exception to the rule, no matter how confident the man, Casanova then proceeded to offer personally tailored insights to each of the cads seated at his table:

David Letterman, Late Night Talk Show Host
Pappagallo! Casanova could only say, "Mai merda dove si mangia," which means in Americano, "Never sh*t where you eat."

Eliot Spitzer, Former New York Governor (Democrat)
Ipocrita! The love gov thought he'd been a big winner all night with his lucky number 9, but Casanova dismissed it as dumb luck inasmuch as the love gov should never have paid for something he could've gotten for free if he'd only played his cards right. The master admonished him to be more cautious the next time he decided to point his finger at others because there would always be three more fingers pointing right back at him. Casanova also suggested he consider leaving the country for a while. Maybe he could lay low in France because they understand about these things in France. Just ask Roman Polanski.

Bill Clinton, Former U.S. President (Democrat)

---

[1] **MUSE WITH BENEFITS, or "MWB" for short.** (Archetype): Not to be mistaken for a musty "MOWB," the MWB customarily proffers distraction with action, arousal without a spousal, hanky-panky with a little spanky, stimulations with few limitations, thrills with skills, flings with no strings, tantalization without penalization, tease then a please between the sheets, and lastly, creative snippets after a few whip its. As would be expected, the MWB tends to attract the greedy (and not necessarily the needy), and we all know who they are ... those who just have to have more, even after snatching up everything else.

Don Giovanni! The world's greatest lover felt like he was looking in the mirror when his eyes came to rest upon Bill Clinton. He could've chided Bill a little about that blue dress fiasco, but frankly, he just didn't think he could teach Bill anything Bill didn't already know. In fact, Bill could probably teach him a thing or two. He suggested they have a private tête-à-tête when his shift was over to compare memoirs.

Mark Sanford, South Carolina Governor (Republican)
Imbecille! Don't cry for me Argentina. And soul mate? Casanova was confused. What's love got to do with it? Then referred him to "ImaRAKE" Step 4.

John Edwards, Former North Carolina Governor (Democrat)
Stupido! Never get caught with the evidence, and that especially includes leaving your DNA behind. Then referred him to "ImaRAKE" Step 4.

Newt Gingrich, Former Speaker of the House (Republican)
Stronzo! Stronzo! Stronzo! Casanova logically understood the marital strategies of a power hungry social climber, yet he warned the man with the reptilian eyes of a water lizard against letting that power go straight to his engorged head. Not one to judge his fellow rakes too overtly, Casanova couldn't help but silently wonder if the stepping stone wives really believed that kissing the toad would turn it into a prince.

Larry Craig, Former Idaho Senator (Republican)
Signore Craig didn't stick around long enough for Casanova to speak insightful words to him like the others. When Casanova directed his attention toward him, he simply stood up from the table, took a wide stance, and slipped Casanova a note wrapped within several large bills as a generous gratuity for the master

before walking away. The note read, "Meet me in the men's room at midnight."

On that note, Casanova looked up as Signore Craig moved to leave the room, and it was then he noticed the throng of starving seekers who were gathered by the thousands – the Moby Dicks[1], the LAB-Rats[2], the Trolls[3], the greedy, and more – all lined up

---

[1] **MOBY DICK** (Archetype): A **male** "MOWB" and a name sometimes used to refer to Ex-VP Dick Cheney. **MOLDY OLD WHITE BREAD, or "MOWB"** (Archetype): A tasty depiction of a human anachronism who routinely derives sustenance from stale, inedible, and moldy ways of thinking, while advocating modus operandi that is firmly entrenched in standards set by the "Old Guard." MOWBs are not conservatively categorized or necessarily stereotyped by gender, age, race, culture, or even political party affiliation; but usually reveal their unmistakable MOWB-ness with a mindset deeply rooted in entitlement, arrogance, superiority and double standards.

[2] **LAB-RAT** (Archetype): These are the fringe skulkers who hover just below the radar – like they're there but not really part of anything. They appear to be pleasant and normal and give the illusion of making some sort of contribution, yet underneath they're really cold fish with no true need for emotional substance or interpersonal depth. LAB-Rats navigate within a highly compartmentalized world that revolves solely around them which manifests itself in the form of brain-body incongruencies. It's almost as if some unseen master has strategically placed remote-controlled electronic stimulus patches all over their body and knows just when to trigger the switch. This brain-body disconnect gives them little instinct for even the most rudimentary consideration for the needs of another, resulting in a narcissistic drive to achieve their goals at any cost, without conscience or accountability. Busy scurrying and always on the go, and clearly no time for quiet introspection sans distraction, LAB-Rats can frequently be found flying the redeye from L.A. to Boston and back again with Blackberry in hand and a GPS perpetually connected to the unseen master. Evasive and duplicitous by nature, they might even tell you they live in France.

[3] **TROLL ON THE BRIDGE, or "TROLL" for short** (Archetype): These are the corporate-minded gatekeepers who block your every effort to maneuver around them and get across the bridge. This is occasionally done maliciously and without conscience, but more often than not, the blockade is enforced without the Troll even comprehending on a conscious level that it is "the hold-up" – the obstruction blocking all passage to the other side. Since Trolls often believe themselves infallible and eagerly seek to have that belief validated, they usually insist on some sort of ego caressing homage as payment before they'll finally step aside and let you pass them by. And as they smugly wallow in their self-induced position of power by being "the hold-up," Trolls are sadly ignorant to

along the corridor waiting for their chance to play tomcat baccarat.

And then we woke up and realized that despite modern man's pretense of civilized evolvement, the primitive instincts are still running the show, and the show apparently must go on ... even if the ending is always the same. Perhaps it's time we finally change the channel. Who's got the universal remote?

---

the unmistakable, yet ironic fact that they're usually standing in their own way and blocking their own progress as well.

55

The Art Of Reality
Dream Sequence, November 29, 2009

We had a dream ... and in that dream we found ourselves strolling through the surreal terrain of Dutch renaissance painter, Hieronymus Bosch, in "The Garden of Earthly Delights," and felt as though we were immersed in a modern reality feature film that only Tim Burton could direct.

Our voyage through this intoxicating dreamscape plunged us without thought of consequence deep into a world of art imitating life imitating art. To a place where we were incapable of separating fact from fantasy, for the reality is that there was no difference.

And like every true pageant of the masters where a two dimensional painting is brought to real life, we watched like voyeurs as the indulgent derangement of earthly pleasures before us morphed into a third panel reality war zone.

The reality wars being waged within our dream were inescapably dominated by the Balloon Boy[1] posse and the D.C. No R.S.V.P.[2] party crashers. We were rendered speechless as both competitors deliberately left in their wake a smoldering third scene battlefield

---

[1] **BALLOON BOY HOAX** of October 15, 2009 when a homemade helium-filled balloon shaped to resemble a silver flying saucer was released above Fort Collins, Colorado by attention seeking parents who claimed their 6-year-old son was trapped inside it.
[2] **"THE REAL HOUSEWIVES OF D.C."** reality show performers, Michaele and Tareq Salahi, attended an Obama Administration White House dinner as uninvited guests after showing up with an uninvited film crew on November 24, 2009, even passing through two White House security checkpoints, which resulted in security and legal investigations.

fully decimated by outrageous exploits – all dramatically delivered with the flamboyance required of a successful reality show audition. A couple sets of felonious fingerprints were left behind in the scorched earth as well, with perhaps a couple more to follow.

Apparently in the real world, the end is meant to justify the means. This ostensibly translates for many to mean no rules, no boundaries, no limitations, no dignity and usually no talent. So when we see that big reality bull burst into a stampede through the china closet of innocent bystanders and carelessly shatter lives and livelihoods while screaming, "Me! Me! Me!" we've bizarrely come to accept that even bad publicity is still publicity.

Well, psychology 101 has long asserted that negative attention is better than no attention at all. Yet, to repetitively reward the bad behavior of attention grabbers with the media attention they're aggressively hungering for has not only helped create a ravenous monster always starving for attention, but has unquestionably sustained it.

As narcissism continues its incessant me-parade across our high definition screens, and Pavlovian conditioning reinforces the belief that anything and everything goes in the insatiable quest for notoriety, we can only wonder when going too far will just be going too far.

And then we woke up and realized that Bosch's vivid, yet surprisingly realistic, illustration of life's temptations and the human condition has lost no relevance with the passing of time and civilizations. Can we reasonably expect the master's real life garden of earthly delights to remain as relevant in the coming centuries as it is today?

56

Walled Off
Dream Sequence, January 24, 2010

We had a dream ... and in that dream we took our need to know to a new level when we initiated a Google internet search on the subject of CHINA. Given the recent rumblings relative to China's economic seduction of the international investor heavyweights, it seemed a little prudence and due diligence might be in order before taking our currency on a cruise up the ¥angtze River with the big boys.

Accustomed to receiving an uninhibited flow of information at the speed of now, we were predictably confounded when our Google search yielded nothing but a blank white page. And no matter how many times we hit the 'refresh' button and blinked our eyes in disbelief, it was undeniable – a blank page was all we were going to get.

Clearly we'd hit a wall and this raised a big RED flag.

What we already knew (without the benefit of a Google search) was that the world at large has long considered the Great Wall of China to be one of the wonders of the world, yet our dreamtime search results drove us straight into what many are now calling the Great Firewall of China. Erected upon an onerous and non-negotiable platform of cyberspace censorship, evidently this Great Firewall is so towering that China's own Olympic hurdle jumper, Liu Xiang, isn't even able to make the great leap forward and over the top.

For centuries the old proverb, "knowledge is power," has historically encouraged those in the know to wisely acquire (and hopefully share) vast knowledge with the promise of power as a dangled payoff. While this belief system may still prove viable, or perhaps produce the necessary credentials for some spheres of influence, the 21st century adaptation of this old philosophy seems to be more akin to, "money is power."

So as we sit back and watch China overtake Japan as the world's 2nd biggest economy, we can only remind ourselves that information imperialism not only owns our debt, but someone has to keep Wal-Mart in business.

We couldn't sit back and watch for long, however, because something was rotten in the state of our world close to home. And the stench was so foul, even pinching our nostrils shut proved futile against the pungent sulfuric fumes that reeked of rotten eggs and threatened to overtake us. Frankly, we weren't sure what smelled worse – the corrosive gases seeping from the "cheap" toxic drywall lining the walls of our home, or the doggie doo in the backyard laced with remnants of the plastic fillers that had been covertly baked into the dog's food. All with manufacturing labels that read "Made in China."

As if the assault on our noses wasn't bad enough, this dream-now-nightmare directed our eyes to the innumerable infants who were innocently consuming formula mixed from tainted milk powder while snuggled warmly in their highly flammable jumpers. Then on to the toddlers and children who were adorned in dainty jewelry cast out of cadmium while playing in a trance on the floor with toys painted in the vibrant colors only a lead palette can produce. The colors of those toys were almost as brilliant as the countless tubes of lipstick and eye shadow compacts we saw filling bathroom drawers everywhere.

We briefly considered taking a couple of Tylenols for the headache we'd gotten from the toxic drywall fumes, but figured it too was probably made in China.

And then we woke up with a headache and wondered if Confucius ever said, "Don't be evil.[1]"

As China continues to shroud its Great Wall in smoke and mirrors while aggressively maximizing short term profits with cheap knock offs, and actions that harm humanity and kill healthy competition, we are wont to ask who's keeping it in business?

---

[1] **"DON'T BE EVIL"** was Google's former motto and a phrase once used in its corporate code of conduct.

57

Mount Olympus Chariot Sale
Dream Sequence, February 15, 2010

We had a dream ... and in that dream we saw NBC Television Titan, Jeff Zucker, make the power play of a lifetime when he contrived to buy out Zeus, the King of the Gods himself, and purchase the right to sit upon that mighty throne perched high atop Mount Olympus.

Mr. Zucker's strategic calculations reinforced his empirical belief that buying an Olympic kingdom wasn't going to be cheap. Fortunately for Zucker, however, the Roman emperors of yesteryear had generously provided an historic sampling of time-tested tactics on how to successfully secure popular opinion with just a few celebratory games.

So when this Titan doled out $2 Billion for the exclusive rights to televise the international athletic games played in honor of Zeus, it was simply a means to an end. And a little pre-games warm up didn't hurt in priming the power pump either.

We followed along in dreamy disbelief as J.Z. preemptively engineered the thundering clash between late night television Titans, Conan O'Brien and Jay Leno. In the end, Mr. Z firmly established his incontestable reign as the Peacock King when he churlishly swept Conan away with a $45 Million granite curling stone and tossed him deep into Tartarus until September.

While Zeus and Zucker were battling through the hard core negotiations about who'd be king of the mountain, we watched as the other gods quickly took advantage of the distraction and did some mischief-making of their own with the athletic pawns on the ground.

No one enjoys revelry and merry-making more than the god of parties, Dionysus. Dionysus understandably felt a special kinship with Bode Miller, and made sure that the bad boy of skiing got to party and socialize at an Olympic level. Any media backlash from his boy Bode's off course antics would be synchronistically timed to end with the Big Bang[1].

The divine support offered up to Lindsey Vonn by the goddess of victory, Nike, seemed undeniable. That "Sports Illustrated" cover jinx may have made her a target like Chiron for the poisonous arrow of Hercules, but if Nike wanted to prolong Lindsey's pre-race healing time by messing with the weather a little, then so be it.

As we followed the Olympic flame on its time honored pilgrimage to the winter games in Vancouver, we wondered whether or not the Peacock King would capriciously torch the Olympic broadcasts altogether and replace them with reruns of "The Tonight Show," just because he could.

And then we woke up and thought that maybe the gods knew what they were doing when they created an honorary position for Stephen Colbert on the Olympic sports psychology team. Someone has to keep us entertained, and it won't be Conan.

But what we really want to know is who will be king of the mountain and take home the gold?

---

[1] Swiss watch brand Hublot named a special limited edition watch in its Big Bang series after Bode Miller called the "Bode Bang."

58

Greed Takes A Holiday
Dream Sequence, March 3, 2010

We had a dream ... and in that dream we saw Greed standing alone in front of the panoramic window of his imperial penthouse suite perched near the top of The Palm Hotel-Atlantis in Dubai. He gazed out at the glistening Persian Gulf with disconsolation, and tried to shake off the gnawing irritation he felt at the fact that the only palm frond island he could see from his luxurious living room was the Palm Jumeirah.

As Greed stood there, fully saturated in his entitlements, he firmly believed with good reason that only one of anything would simply never be enough. His insatiable heart demanded that he have it all.

And Wall Street was a man after his own heart. Wall Street knew that one of the fastest ways to win the heart of Greed was to bundle up a few derivatives in a red bow, and have them laid on his pillow every evening when his king-sized bed was turned down by the personal maid who never forgot to put that quintessential chocolate crème de menthe on top.

Wall Street owed Greed in a big way for several very banner years, and Wall Street didn't disappoint when it heartily comped Greed's recent holiday junket which included an epicurean Celebrity cruise from his doorstep in Dubai to the Cayman Islands for a little tax free R & R.

Our dream followed Greed to the marina where he boarded a cruise ship that looked to be worthy of him, for it was the biggest and best on the Gulf. Few ships sailing the high seas were elite enough to fly the badge of the Red Shield[1] from its flagpole, and the "Black Pearl" was a flagship indeed.

Every level on the ship prominently housed no less than four ATM cash machines, each boldly sponsored by the Big Four banking buddies whose direct lines were stored on Greed's cell phone speed-dial. He was heartened to see the ATMs on board ship for little could boost the bankers' bottom line faster than weeks of hefty international cash advance fees assessed upon a full boat of high end cruisers. No doubt this Big Four bank-sponsored Greed-junket was long overdue.

As in life, so in love ... er, lust, and never to settle for just one of anything, his evenings were filled with gluttonous options; and since Greed was on holiday, he let his southern head do some of the heavy thinking after sundown. At least until the warm currents of the Indian Ocean carried the ship around the Horn of Africa and into the greedy clutches of the Somalian Pirates[2].

Well, that Red Shield luxury liner may've been too rich for the pirates to pass up, but by the time Greed finished dissecting their bottom line calculations and made it known that his cut wasn't big enough, the pirates couldn't release his ship fast enough. It seems the only real difference that exists between Greed and the Somali Pirates is that Greed doesn't bother to take hostages, yet his tentacles are far reaching and equal opportunity abounds.

---

[1] **RED SHIED**: The Rothschild Banking Family.
[2] **SOMALIAN PIRATES**: The Somali Pirates and their highly lucrative ransom demands were a major threat to international shipping and boating off the Somalian peninsula/Horn of Africa during the war in Somalia from 2006 to 2009. Somalia was considered a failed state until 2012.

And then we woke up and wondered if Bernie[1] ever dreamed about outliving his wife, Ruth, and making Greed the sole beneficiary in his will.

So when Greed comes knocking on your door looking for more, will he be turned away in earnest or will he receive the red carpet treatment he expects?

---

[1] **BERNIE**: Bernard L. Madoff, Chairman and Founder of Bernard L. Madoff Investment Securities LLC, 1960. Arrested on December 11, 2008 and sentenced to 150 years of quiet meditation, Bernie currently (as of 2009) awaits his formal induction into the Ponzi Hall of Fame. AKA: the Jewish Treasury Bill and the new face of Greed. He was formerly a philanthropist, a regular family man about town, and a prominent leader in the financial services industry who gave everyone he was screwing the big KISS (keep it simple, stupid) of financial, and sometimes literal, death.

59

Tea Hee Haw
Dream Sequence, May 20, 2010

We had a dream ... and in that dream we found ourselves standing in the middle of a vast Texas wasteland next to a large cluster of sagebrush that was still dripping from the recent rain storm. The cracked earth that had previously lined the nearby creek bed was now engorged as the rain waters rushed by in a hurry to fill the scrubby pond down yonder.

That was where we first saw Jed-Dubya[1] hunkered down with his locked and loaded rifle, fully poised to pick off the croaking frogs just as fast as they could leap out of the flooding pond.

It looked as if Jed-Dubya's short attention span was about to accidentally be the making of him, for our dream then showed him getting easily distracted by an unidentified shiny object across the pond. And his first reaction, of course, was to shoot at it. He missed, but hit pay dirt for up from the ground came a bubbling crude. Oil, that is. Black gold. Time to throw a Texas Tea Party.

With the help of one Mr. Drysdale of the Red Shield[2] Bank, Jed-Dubya eventually got around to selling his new oil field to the president of the OK Oil Company, Mr. Dick. Mr. Dick had always considered himself to be the biggest fish in a little pond, and

---

[1] **XP "W"**: Ex-President George W. Bush, 43rd President of the United States of America, Inc., officially sworn in to office January 20, 2001. He served two disastrous 4-year terms then finally crashed and burned his way out on January 19, 2009. He was succeeded by The Big BOPR (aka Barack Obama).
[2] **RED SHIELD**: The Rothschild Banking Family

rarely failed to stand a bit taller when afforded the opportunity to introduce himself to big clients with his favorite nickname, Moby.

Dubya naturally saw no need to jump into the middle of the funding fetch with Moby Dick[1] when all the price beatin' could be left in the robust hands of his nephew, JethRush[2]. Heck, before Jed could whittle a whale out of a piece of driftwood, JethRush had strong-armed a deal that saw Moby Dick's right forearm smacked down backward on the table after JethRush had arm rassled it flat like a carnie at the county fair. This is what the kinfolks call, "doin' business on a handshake."

During the weeks that passed between shootin' and sellin', Dubya's velvety oil spewed from the Earth unchecked, and the waters of that scrubby pond turned black and toxic with crude oil. Any frog that had been lucky enough to survive Jed's shooting party was now thickly coated in heavy crude and washed up along the shoreline never to hop again.

Now Jed's ole Granny Armstrong[3] was a rootin' tootin' Texan to the core, and she'd taken an unusual liking to OK Oil's Moby

---

[1] **MOBY DICK** (Archetype): A **male** "MOWB" and a name sometimes used to refer to Ex-VP Dick Cheney. **MOLDY OLD WHITE BREAD, or "MOWB"** (Archetype): A tasty depiction of a human anachronism who routinely derives sustenance from stale, inedible, and moldy ways of thinking, while advocating modus operandi that is firmly entrenched in standards set by the "Old Guard." MOWBs are not conservatively categorized or necessarily stereotyped by gender, age, race, culture, or even political party affiliation; but usually reveal their unmistakable MOWB-ness with a mindset deeply rooted in entitlement, arrogance, superiority and double standards.

[2] **RUSH LIMBAUGH**: Limbaugh was an opinionated, loud and outspoken American conservative political commentator who hosted "The Rush Limbaugh Show" radio show from 1988 until his death in 2021. He was arrested for prescription drug fraud in 2006 due, in part, to his addiction to painkillers; OxyContin being a particular favorite.

[3] **ANNE L. ARMSTRONG**: Armstrong was a Republican politician from Texas who also served as a U.S. Diplomat during the Ford and Carter Administrations. She died in July, 2008. In February, 2006 Dick Cheney "accidentally" shot retired

Dick. Granny Armstrong offered Mr. Dick a rare invitation to do some big game huntin' on the ranch before it was all packed up. Good thing Granny was an M.D. too cuz it sure came in handy when Moby Dick unwittingly took a pot shot at the Texas law man who'd only joined the hunt to flush out Jed's baby girl and the county's hottest looker, Elly May Palin[1], from behind the bushes where she was busy winkin' at all them critters running for their lives.

As soon as Jed-Dubya had securely deposited his copious bounty in the Red Shield Bank, it was time to load up the truck and move to Washington D.C. Thanks once more to the tacit manipulation of Mr. Drysdale, Jed-Dubya was able to buy up the biggest White House that Pennsylvania Avenue had to offer. When the seller couldn't afford to pay its underwater mortgage to China, let alone the back taxes, it was without a doubt the best deal the new century had to offer.

Dubya was thrilled. He had the whittling porch of his dreams. But poor Granny Armstrong. She just wasn't sure what to do about that huge steeple facing the long cement pond that was taking up too much space on her green grassroots backyard so richly enhanced with astroturf.

As far as Moby Dick was concerned, JethRush had found his calling. Whenever Mr. Dick would throw one of those regular

---

Texas attorney, Harry Whittington, with his shotgun during a quail hunt on the Armstrong Ranch in Riviera, TX.
[1] **SARAH PALIN**: Palin was the former Governor of Alaska from 2006 until 2009, when she resigned before finishing her term. She was the 2008 VP running mate of Republican Presidential candidate, John McCain. Palin had a reputation for making up words during her speeches, and often referred to herself as a Maverick, a Rogue, a Ronald Reagan devotee, and sometimes as a "Pitbull with Lipstick" when at hockey games. She also claimed that she could see Russia from her house.

White House Tea Parties he was wont to have for our friendly neighborhood OPEC drillers, the party would invariably conclude in the parlor with a little JethRush price fixin' "handshake" shake-down. And every once in a while, M. D. would even secretly arrange for JethRush to do some big pharma-rasslin' with his good buddies over at the OxyContin dispensary, just because he could. No pain, no gain.

JethRush's kissin' cuzin, Elly May, had her own common sense solution for growing Pa's oil empire, and family values would firmly govern her grand plan which was steamrolling forward nicely under the rally cry, "Drill, baby, drill!" Elly May couldn't wait to grab her Uzi and jump on board the Exxon Valdez for a tanker cruise along the pipeline to Alaska. What she didn't expect to see on the expedition were all of those trees. A tree's a tree. How many more do you need to look at? Oh! – Oh! - OH!! Maybe the family should think about expanding into the lumber business. **wink*~*wink**

And then we woke up and realized that even when the body appears to be running around without a head, it always seems to get where it's headed. We can only wonder now where the Tea Party is headed next.

Y'all come back for tea now, ya hear?

Tea Hee Haw Sing Along

A companion sing along and hootenanny for "TEA HEE HAW."

A "Vice Versa Verses[1]" parody to be sung to the tune of "The Ballad of Jed Clampett" (written by Paul Henning); also known as the theme song from "The Beverly Hillbillies."

"HILLBILLY HIGH TEA"

Come and join a party Jed-Dubya once led,
A simpleton his pappy had silver spoon fed,
Shootin' for some way to ease his aimless mood,
While steepin' in the ground rich Texas tea brewed.

Oil that is. Black gold. Texas tea party.

---

[1] **VICE VERSA VERSES (VVV):** The "Rhymin' Ivan" version of a "Dream Sequence."

Well, JethRush's arm rasslin' made Jed a billionaire,
And Drysdale said, "time to party in our lair,"
Said, "the Oval Office is the place you oughtta be,"
So they packed up the truck and moved to Wash D.C.

N. O. that is. Beauty queens. FOX knows news.

Well scrap all yer plans, let the grassroots march begin
Do the hokey pokey with yer pickets and Palin,
Moby gets a handshake from the folks who come to tea,
And serves a heapin' helpin' of more fear and panicky.

O. K. that is. Bottomless pit. Come stub yer toes on the 'turf.

Y'all come back for tea now, ya hear?

60

More Moves To Dominate The World
Dream Sequence, October 4, 2010

We had a dream ... and in that dream we found ourselves struggling alongside a working class crew trying to regain control of a schooner bounty that had initially been charted for Atlantic City, but was instead violently blown off course, rudder snapping in a lurch. We heard the tattered sails shutter with purpose as the hull heaved and bobbed directionless through ravenous waters that grew more dangerous with each billowing swell.

No one saw it coming. Or at least that's what they all said. It was as if the atmosphere had turned on a dime, right about the time the East Wind began squalling with subversion. One minute we were coasting through prosperous trade routes on confident sails bloated with warm sea breezes, not a storm cloud in sight; and the next saw our ship taking on water so fast that sinking appeared inevitable.

As we scurried to bail out the water one bucket at a time, we never even noticed the growing wall of water that was mobilizing to put us in our place. And when that financial tsunami finally got our full attention was when it capsized our boat without remorse somewhere in the middle of the Devil's Triangle, where it dumped us unceremoniously into a very rough sea without so much as a safety net.

We managed to keep our heads above water just long enough to see a monstrous whale the size of China circle and descend with rapacious jaws intent upon swallowing us up.

Our dream then dropped us deep within the belly of the whale where we could hear the reverberating voices of those trapped around us long before we could actually see them.

From the surrounding conversation, we soon learned that the whale had a name, ¥uaning More, although the group regularly referred to it as simply "MORE."

The more we listened, the more we understood how much MORE prided itself on being the hardest working predator in the sea. It thrived on the chaos that comes from war and ruin, and there was no time for rest because voracious accumulation is a 24/7 enterprise. MORE was cleverly adroit at tickling desperate ears with politeness and dangled promises, a master in the fine art of bait and switch, and not above making thy neighbor beg. Apparently MORE honored only one golden rule – "he who has the gold, makes the rules" – and this rule seemed to justify MORE's refusal to play by anyone's rules but its own.

When our eyes finally adjusted to the darkness that held us hostage, we became better acquainted with our fellow captives, including a few Pleasure Island castaways.

Wall Street GetOver
This GetOver could do little more than boast about being the original woodcarver, when in fact he was the rainmaker who brought on the storm.

Pinocchio
Pinocchio had always dreamed of having a life with no strings, and MORE had slyly seduced him into thinking he could have his cadmium and eat it too. Well, someone once said that Pinocchio was Italian for a reason, and this Pinocchio had absolutely no intention of ever being made in China, for he had a plan. A

strategy designed to beat MORE at its own game. Pinocchio figured that the more he lied, the longer his nose would get, until eventually its length would allow him to pry open the jaws of MORE just enough to slip away relatively unscathed.

Caracas Cricket[1]
No matter how hard he tried to stop the incessant chirping, Caracas Cricket just couldn't keep his knees from rubbing everyone the wrong way. He spent most of his chirping hours looking up through MORE's blowhole into the night sky as he wished upon the stars for higher oil prices and for someone to rub just a little bit of that oil between his knees.

StromRuski[2]
Someone has to pull the strings behind the biggest show on Earth and StromRuski believed himself to be the perfect puppet master.

Goodluck Jonah[3] and his simpleton sidekick GideGaddafi[4]
Goodluck Jonah may have gotten his start as Honest John but he realized pretty early on that honesty wasn't what put him on the winning side, it was self-made luck. And GideGaddafi was a blustering windbag who'd shown himself to be an agreeable feline comrade because he was agile enough to blow in the direction of any winning wind and still land on his feet.

---

[1] VENEZUELA, **Hugo Chavez**, Former President.
[2] RUSSIA, **Vladimir Putin**, President. And Still Is ...
[3] NIGERIA, **Goodluck Jonathan**, Former President.
[4] LIBYA, **Colonel Muammar Gaddafi**, Dictator. U.S. Secretary of State, Hillary Clinton's 2011 quote about Gaddafi, "we came, we saw, he died."

AhmadineDonkey[1]

Had it not been for that obnoxious braying which never seemed to stop, we probably wouldn't have even noticed AhmadineDonkey sulking off on the side alone. Someone lurking behind MORE's ribcage tried to shut him up by throwing out a few USB worms which he gobbled up with gusto. The braying thankfully stopped when AhmadineDonkey began instead to hawk up stuxnet code, then proceeded to vocally reproduce "myrtus, myrtus, myrtus, ..." without control.

Mingling amongst the group ensnared by MORE's bottomless pit were plenty of other nameless naughty boys in business suits who'd been sucked in from every nation throughout the world. "But I run a business," they all declared defensively, "if somebody's buying, I'm selling." Apparently that's their story and they're sticking to it.

And then we woke up and realized that when we whittle away at our own foundation, the structure will invariably weaken and the resulting gaps will beg to be filled with MORE.

After all of this we can't help wondering, does the Blue Fairy really have the power to turn those trapped inside the belly of the whale into true human beings?

---

[1] IRAN, **Mahmoud Ahmadinejad**, Former President.

61

Which View Is Witch?
Dream Sequence, October 29, 2010

We had a dream ... and in that dream we found ourselves stepping over a troll bridge into the enchanted woods of Winterthur with nothing but the moon to light our way. The forbidden faerie ring to our right was veiled in a thick midnight mist and slipped by unnoticed as the spirits of the woods urged us forward along a serpentine pathway.

It was the eerie sound of chanting, emanating from deep in the mist that stopped us dead in our tracks.

Our dream then took a sharp right, off the beaten path, in the direction of the faerie ring where a yellow light was faintly glowing through the heavy haze. We sucked in our breath when we eventually caught sight of the chantress, and then we quietly crouched, hiding in the shadows of a mushroom to witness with morbid fascination her clandestine mid-term ritual.

While it should've come as no surprise for us to witness the magick making of Christine O'Donnell[1] since she'd undoubtedly managed to cast a spell over the people of Delaware, it's just that we never really expected to catch her in the act in the woods.

---

[1] **CHRISTINE O'DONNELL**: O'Donnell ran on the GOP ticket to replace Joe Biden as Senator of Delaware in 2010 with strong financial support from the Republican Tea Party movement and an endorsement from Sarah Palin. She usurped 9-term incumbent, Michael Castle, in the primary but lost the race to Democratic candidate, Chris Coons. She received national media attention for a campaign advertisement where she declared, "I am not a witch." She also had no problem telling Castle during the primary that "this wasn't a bake-off" and to "get his man pants on" in response to what she believed was un-manly behavior in his campaign tactics. Her father was an actor who was a stand-in for Bozo the Clown on occasion.

Well, God works in mysterious ways and Christine truly believed she could secretly help Him help her win that seat in the Senate. And it sure helped that no one had ever officially mandated there be any separation between church and state. It also helped that she was a member of the FOXy Palin[1] coven. This gave her the benefit of a direct line to the spirit of Ronald Reagan, and if an astrological roadmap could help him successfully navigate a presidency, then the Book of Shadows could certainly help her sideline all of the challengers and critics she'd encountered on the way to Washington.

In a rare "Ah-Ha!" moment, Christine realized the best way to render her detractors impotent would be to simply change their point of view.

On an altar dripping in blue hen's blood laid O'Donnell's opened spell book, brilliantly lit by an arc of five blazing black candles. Next to the altar stood Christine, glistening with sweat in a red business suit, busily working her magick while stirring the bubbling cauldron before her with focused intent. Her spellbinding witches' brew appeared to be a simmering mixture of rich milk, sweet goldenrod, peach blossoms and holly berries, potently finished off with a transformational pinch of Delaware's DuPont chemicals. The heat from the fire beneath the pot was so intense that it even reached out to sear us in the shadows.

---

[1] **SARAH PALIN**: Palin was the former Governor of Alaska from 2006 until 2009, when she resigned before finishing her term. She was the 2008 VP running mate of Republican Presidential candidate, John McCain. Palin had a reputation for making up words during her speeches, and often referred to herself as a Maverick, a Rogue, a Ronald Reagan devotee, and sometimes as a "Pitbull with Lipstick" when at hockey games. She also claimed that she could see Russia from her house.

Like the five points on a pentagram, we watched as Christine O'Donnell commanded the spirits of her naysayers to spend one episode inside the bodies of the five women of "The View."

Dick Cheney got to feel with heavy dreads the "caring" heartbeat of **Whoopi Goldberg.**

Bill O'Reilly[1] got to watch his pinhead explode through the "patriotic" eyes of **Joy Behar.**

Karl Rove[2] got to learn how to skillfully navigate America's crossroads with dignity through the filtered lens of **Barbara Walters.**

Mike Castle got to taste the bitterness of defeat on the "gracious" tongue of **Sherri Shepard.**

Eric Cantor[3] got to shoot off his young gun while trying not to repeat the mistakes of the past as he admired a body that

---

[1] **BILL O'REILLY**: O'Reilly was a conservative political commentator, journalist and former host of "The O'Reilly Factor" on the FOX news channel from 1996 to 2017. A prolific author, he published "Pinheads and Patriots: Where You Stand in the Age of Obama" in 2010 and was a frequent opinionated, outspoken and divisive late night talk show guest during this time.

[2] **KARL ROVE**: Rove was known to be a Republican political consultant, policy advisor and lobbyist in his role as Senior Advisor and Deputy Chief of Staff during the administration of President George W. Bush, resigning this role in August, 2007. Rove vigorously defended the Bush administration's use of torture known as waterboarding. He founded "American Crossroads" in 2010, a U.S. Super PAC that raises funds from "secret" donors to advocate for certain chosen Republican candidates. American Crossroads devised many new methods of corporate fundraising that were opened up by the Supreme Court's "Citizens United" ruling.

[3] **ERIC CANTOR**: Cantor was a Republican politician who represented the state of Virginia in the House of Representatives from 2001 to 2014. He was one of three founding members of the "GOP Young Guns Program" and in 2010, he wrote a bestselling book with his co-founders called "Young Guns, A New

reminded him of his feminine side, and obviously, **Elizabeth Hasselbeck**.

Their special guest that day was Alec Baldwin who happened to know the five ladies of "The View" well enough to recognize when they weren't themselves. And when Mike Castle in Sherri's voice asked Alec to define what it meant to be unmanly, Alec quipped with annoyance that this was not a bake off and suggested that Mike go get his man-pants on. As Alec stormed off the set, stage left, he snidely told the others in passing to man-up.

And then we woke up and realized that anyone raised by Bozo the Clown has some pretty big shoes to fill; and just because one acts like a clown, doesn't necessarily mean they don't have the instincts of a fox.

Have we too just been given a new view of extremism?

Generation of Conservative Leaders." He was known in 2010 to work with the Tea Party movement in his 7th congressional district.

62

Billz Above
Dream Sequence, January 12, 2011

We had a dream ... and in that dream we found ourselves trapped deep within the thronging temple of temptation known as New York City's Times Square as XP "W"[1] shouted down a fiery sermon from the heavens above via skyscraping Jumbo-Trons, proclaiming, "People! Spend more to save America, and you too, shall be saved!"

The mesmerized crowd around us stared upward as every subconscious mind on Times Square hypnotically absorbed the almighty message meant to mobilize them into martyrdom and saving the world with excessive consumption without thought of the cost.

Just when it seemed the crowd had been fully converted to consume without consequence, the sound of music started to reverberate loudly off of the buildings bordering the Square. Millions of glassy eyes dropped to watch as the "Not Buying It Band" began to march into Times Square from 42nd Street flamboyantly followed by the Reverend Billy[2] and his "Stop Shopping Gospel Choir" who were singing out their "Stop Shopping" theme song as if our very souls depended on it.

Our dream then showed the crowd's truth-seeking migration toward the televangelist front-man for the "Church of Life After

---

[1] **XP "W"**: Ex-President George W. Bush, 43rd President of the United States of America, Inc. officially sworn in to office January 20, 2001. Served two disastrous 4-year terms then finally crashed and burned his way out on January 19, 2009. He was succeeded by The Big BOPR (aka Barack Obama).
[2] **REVEREND BILLY and the Church of Stop Shopping**: www.RevBilly.com

Shopping" to hear what this proselyte had to say. The Reverend Billy was not only a man who looked like Elvis, talked like Elvis, but refused to shop like Elvis; he was a man with a serious, life-changing message.

Reverend Billy declared us to be in the midst of the "Shopocalypse," and he wasn't talking fire and brimstone. It was time, according to the Reverend, to slay the dragon and replace the Devil's holy days of Black Friday and Boxing Day with sanctioned boycotts and "Buy Nothing" days.

When the crowd began to jeer and hurl their credit cards at him in protest, Reverend Billy's body lurched forward without warning; then it began to writhe and shake uncontrollably as he lapsed into a credit card exorcism by way of response. As the exorcism wound down, the crowd shifted and moved into sheepish retreat with their recovered credit cards – CRV codes irretrievably obscured and PIN numbers permanently erased from memory.

And then we woke up and realized that we've been sold down the river. And we're not talking trickle down.

Apparently the bill of goods we've been sold has strategically passed the buck onto the credit card balances of those who can least afford it by seducing them into thinking that they must buy, buy, and buy some more in order to save America's economy. Yet, it seems that those with the financial means to put a serious dent in the nation's obscene deficit by simply paying their fair share of tax get to have it both ways because the more the rest of us spend, the higher their bottom line, and the more they get to keep.

What we really want to know, though, is if every citizen were to run their personal finances like corporate America, how would life in America and the economy look then?

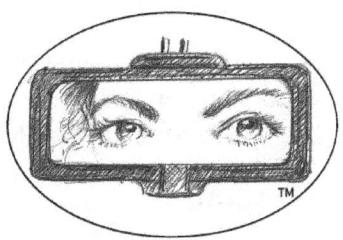

ITRVM Vice Versa Verses

VICE VERSA VERSES (VVV): The "Rhymin' Ivan" version of a "Dream Sequence."

Wedded Biz
Vice Versa Verses
© by DK King

Once upon a time
There was the perfect mate.
Society counsels marry,
That means incorporate.
Articles and by-laws
Once duly created,
Form a household compliant
And lawfully regulated.
Board meets for nuptials recited
As both in agreement converge.
Separate assets become united
In a co-mingled blend 'n merge.

So before you speak the words, "I do,"
You might want to negotiate
The best deal for you.

Commitment phobes
More risk adverse,
Commit to share space
Without sharing their purse.
Companionship is rendered
By indie entrepreneurs.
No autonomy is surrendered,
Shared bennies both procures.
Secerning self-preservement
Proves a win-win strategy,
For freelancing contractors
Circumventing legality.

So before you speak the words, "I do,"
You might want to explore
The options available to you.

Partners opt-in one hundred percent,
Position their investments to grow.
C.F.O. recommendation is buy vs. rent
Before delivering an I.P.O.
Celebration returns every fiscal year end
While hopes and dreams are propagated.
Black bottom line with plenty to spend,
Empty bedrooms soon are populated.
Team players busy multi-tasking,
Fully booked from morning to night,
Fosters synergistic fast tracking
For unions working the system right.

So before you speak the words, "I do,"
You might want to hold in reserve
Something solely for you.

Corporations plan for perpetuity,
Redefining "til death do us part."
Strategic goal is long term security,
As shown on the pension plan pie chart.
Life cycles forth with its ebb and flow,
Branches form a brand name niche.
Years of laying all those ducks in a row,
Not discounting that seven year itch.
Dissolution optional if shareholders split,
"Happily ever after" seems a fairy tale.
The end of the day finds it difficult to quit
When your business is just too big to fail.

So before you speak the words, "I do,"
You might want to ask,
Is marriage the right business for you?

ITRVM DICTIONARY

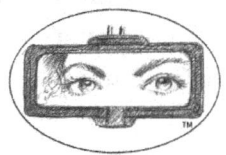

We tend to utilize a vernacular of our own and thought this would help you speak our language too.

B-REX (Archetype): A female "MOWB."

BENNY: Federal Reserve Bank Chairman, Ben S. Bernanke, appointed by President George W. Bush and sworn in February 1, 2006. He was the successor to Alan Greenspan at a time when Atlas Shrugged, and he became 2008's crowned Cannibal King after running Hank (aka Henry S. Paulson, Jr.) off the road.

BERNIE: Bernard L. Madoff, Chairman and Founder of Bernard L. Madoff Investment Securities LLC, 1960. Arrested on December 11, 2008 and sentenced to 150 years of quiet meditation, Bernie currently (as of 2009) awaits his formal induction into the Ponzi Hall of Fame. AKA the Jewish Treasury Bill and the new face of Greed. He was formerly a philanthropist, a regular family man about town, and a prominent leader in the financial services industry who gave everyone he was screwing the big KISS (keep it simple, stupid) of financial, and sometimes literal, death.

BLAGO: Milorad "Rod" R. Blagojevich. He was a record holder as the first Illinois governor to ever be impeached on January 29, 2009. He made sure to jet back to his Chicago home before the Senate's final vote could formalize his civilian status and deprive him of the ride home from Springfield on the state plane. Blago notoriously tried to sell The Big BOPR's (aka Barack Obama) vacated senate seat to the highest bidder and had the misfortune of being wiretapped along the way. While he insisted he was the victim of a rush to judgment, it kinda looks like he did a Nixon and just got caught doing what everyone else has always done. It's all gonna be bleepin' golden in jail.

BUSH FLU: A highly resistant and uncooperative viral strain that was released from the golden parachutes strapped to the backs of financial district CEOs as they were ejected by their Board of Directors and pushed out of Air Force One. Subsequent studies eventually confirmed that the virus was carried and transmitted through the small air-borne drops of crude oil that leeched from the edges of the golden parachutes upon deployment. Symptoms include: Great Depression. No money in the bank. Your bank's ATM machine holds your debit card hostage and instead spits out a government I.O.U. by way of a receipt in the form of Federal Reserve Notes.

BUSH-WHACKED: 1) We play and you get to pay. 2) Shootin' from the hip into dead space and living with the consequences of someone else's good idea for you that has essentially no basis in reality, no vision, no foresight. You know, like a bad blind date that goes nowhere fast, and yet somehow, you're left holding the check. 3) 21st Century synonym for "it's my way or the highway." 4) Cronyism.

DADDY WARBUCKS: Warren E. Buffett, CEO of Berkshire Hathaway, who has been considered at times to be the richest man in the world. AKA the fox put in charge of the chicken coop, and the inspiration for The BIG BOPR's (aka Barack Obama) "Buffett Rule." Although Daddy Warbucks won't officially endorse his namesake "Buffett Rule," we'll always remember that he was the slyest fox of all by suggesting that all the other rich foxes pay a proper tax.

DREAM SEQUENCE (DS): An ITRVM Allegory where we weave things together that don't seem to go together to create a vision of things to come. We liken these to random, off-road detours along the lookout ledge of our own private Idaho. We also like to call these "Crazy Ivans."

GOP: GENDER OVERLORD PARTY, or "The New GOP" for short (A Cultural Mindset): The "GOP" acronym known for centuries in the United States to stand for the Republican "Grand Old Party" has been updated to be the new signifier for the "Gender Overlord Party." This turn of the 21st century revision was made in order to better reflect the bullying nature and evolving cultural mindset of a GOP that has elected to stand on a platform righteously rooted in conflict, contradiction and condescension.

HANK: 74th Secretary of the Treasury, Henry S. Paulson, Jr., nominated by President George W. Bush in June, 2006. He was the former Chairman and CEO of Goldman Sachs. AKA the 2008 Cannibal King contender who was overtaken by Benny (aka Ben S. Bernanke) and swiftly ran off the road, but at least he managed to save Goldman Sachs after the crash.

I-ROB: John A. Thain, former CEO of Merrill Lynch who resigned on January 22, 2009, right before Bank of America CEO Ken Lewis could sack him. Mr. Fix-It proposed the shotgun wedding between Merrill and BofA and their CEOs, which abruptly ended in annulment barely 3 months later (didn't something like that happen with Rene' Zellweger and Kenny Chesney?). BofA gobbled up Merrill's enormous deficit and naturally passed the tab on to the taxpayers in the form of TARP bailout funding. I-ROB smoothly managed to expend $1.22 Million to make his office feel more like home, and to secretly disburse $4 Billion in early employee bonuses before dashing off to Vail, Colorado for a year-end ski holiday just as Merrill's $15.3 Billion 2008 4Q loss was announced. AKA "I-ROBOT" for his mechanical coldness, void of emotion and intense financial focus.

LAB-RAT (Archetype): These are the fringe skulkers who hover just below the radar – like they're there but not really part of anything. They appear to be pleasant and normal and give the illusion of making some sort of contribution, yet underneath they're really cold fish with no true need for emotional substance or interpersonal depth. LAB-Rats navigate within a highly compartmentalized world that revolves solely around them which manifests itself in the form of brain-body incongruencies. It's almost as if some unseen master has strategically placed remote-controlled electronic stimulus patches all over their body and knows just when to trigger the switch. This brain-body disconnect gives them little instinct for even the most rudimentary consideration for the needs of another, resulting in a narcissistic drive to achieve their goals at any cost, without conscience or accountability. Busy scurrying and always on the go, and clearly no time for quiet introspection sans distraction, LAB-Rats can frequently be found flying the redeye from L.A. to Boston and back again with Blackberry in hand and a GPS perpetually connected to the unseen master. Evasive and duplicitous by nature, they might even tell you they live in France.

MOBY DICK (Archetype): A **male** "MOWB," and a name sometimes used to refer to Ex-VP Dick Cheney.

MOLDY OLD WHITE BREAD, or "MOWB" (Archetype): A tasty depiction of a human anachronism who routinely derives sustenance from stale, inedible, and moldy ways of thinking, while advocating modus operandi that is firmly entrenched in standards set by the "Old Guard." MOWBs are not conservatively categorized or necessarily stereotyped by gender, age, race, culture, or even political party affiliation; but usually reveal their unmistakable MOWB-ness with a mindset deeply rooted in entitlement, arrogance, superiority and double standards.

MUSE WITH BENEFITS, or "MWB" for short. (Archetype): Not to be mistaken for a musty "MOWB," the MWB customarily proffers distraction with action, arousal without a spousal, hanky-panky with a little spanky, stimulations with few limitations, thrills with skills, flings with no strings, tantalization without penalization, tease then a please between the sheets, and lastly, creative snippets after a few whip its. As would be expected, the MWB tends to attract the greedy (and not necessarily the needy), and we all know who they are … those who just have to have more, even after snatching up everything else.

RAHMBO: Rahm Emanuel, former White House Chief of Staff for The Big BOPR (aka Barack Obama); and prior to that he was a Member of the U.S. House of Representatives for Illinois' 5th Congressional District. He survived the D.C. lion's den and left the lair on September 30, 2010 to pursue his dream of being at the clandestine beck and call of The Big BOPR, or maybe even Chicago's new mayor for life.

RED SHIELD: The Rothschild Banking Family.

THE BIG BOPR: Barack Obama, President and "Renegade" (his Secret Service code name). He was the successor to President George W. Bush (aka XP "W") after being "sworn" in to office on January 20, 2009 as the 44th President of the United States of America, Inc. AKA Traitor 44.

TROLL ON THE BRIDGE, or "TROLL" for short (Archetype): These are the corporate-minded gatekeepers who block your every effort to maneuver around them and get across the bridge. This is occasionally done maliciously and without conscience, but more often than not, the blockade is enforced without the Troll even comprehending on a conscious level that it is "the hold-up" – the obstruction blocking all passage to the other side. Since Trolls often believe themselves infallible and eagerly seek to have that belief validated, they usually insist on some sort of ego caressing homage as payment before they'll finally step aside and let you pass them by. And as they smugly wallow in their self-induced position of power by being "the hold-up," Trolls are sadly ignorant to the unmistakable, yet ironic fact that they're usually standing in their own way and blocking their own progress as well.

VICE VERSA VERSES (VVV): The "Rhymin' Ivan" version of a "Dream Sequence."

VULTURE CULTURE (A Cultural Mindset): The Vulture Culture is a parasitical cultural mindset that encourages self-serving individuals to collectively devour the flesh right off of the bones of society like a wake of New World Vultures gathering to feast on the susceptible. Those immersed in today's Vulture Culture tend to personify the gladiatorial spirit of "winner takes all;" and like the competitive arenas of ancient Rome where the sole objective of the properly indoctrinated gladiator is to win at any cost, every victory sustained is the direct result of cutthroat competition on steroids. There are no rules, there are no hostages. There is only winning. In this myopic quest to win, disciples of the Vulture Culture think nothing of pissing all over everything they step on, and the corrosive uric acid that rolls down their legs unchecked does little more than leave in its wake a wide trail of scorched earth. Those belonging to the Vulture Culture have absolutely no desire to contribute anything new or of value to the very society they feed on. They prefer instead to feed upon the remains of the day like scavengers, for what they lack in creative innovation, they make up for in carnage.

WHITE MINIVAN (Theory): This is a theory which basically asserts that nothing good ever comes from a White Minivan. When you notice that the flow of traffic is inexplicably interrupted, just look ahead, and discover for yourself that invariably the source of the hold-up is a White Minivan. Examples demonstrate it best: 1. Stopped in the carpool lane while the cars in every other lane whoosh by with the speed of light? Try to look beyond the gigantic SUV in front of you and see who's at the head of the line – bet it's a White Minivan. 2. Have you ever found yourself humming with the flow of freeway traffic when out of nowhere comes that White Minivan from the fast lane who's just realized it's about to miss the off-ramp it needs in an 1/8th of a mile, as you speechlessly witness it cut off all 4 lanes of traffic (including your own and the semi's) just in time to make that exit, and with 1/16th of a mile to spare? 3. Stopped at a signal, sandwiched in with mouth agape, when the White Minivan in front of you backs up straight into your front bumper with its projecting trailer hitch (leaving a very un-aerodynamic hole in its wake) because it didn't think anyone was behind it and it wanted to turn around without driving around the block? (And yes, we have had this happen). Get the idea? Our observational research thus far supports the belief that this theory applies to large White Vans and most White SUVs as well. **Side Mirror** Footnote: White Minivans typically run in packs with other minivans, and they tend to herd or congregate around school parking lots and the shopping centers of suburbia. These suburban parking lot gatherings take on a surreal life of their own (not far from Stepford) in an asphalt dimension called the "Land of the Minivan."

XP "W": Ex-President George W. Bush, 43rd President of the United States of America, Inc. officially sworn in to office January 20, 2001. He served two disastrous 4-year terms then finally crashed and burned his way out on January 19, 2009. He was succeeded by The Big BOPR (aka Barack Obama).

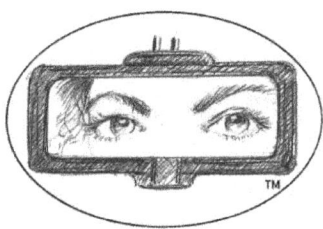

We've come to **THE END** of this road trip, time travelers.

About The Authors

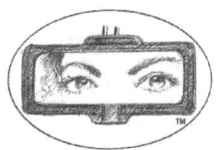

DK King

A born storyteller of Irish American descent, **DK King** brings to the written page a refreshing, unique, and embracing style of literary art that captivates the reader with a relevant, yet visionary, mixture of wit and wisdom.

DK began sharing her sagacious style of writing in 2008 with the creation of a collaborative blog called "**In The Rear View Mirror**," along with Artist, KAd Collins. In 2010, she created her own personal blog where she featured condensed raw snippets of her life experiences in Big Sky Country, Montana as she prepared to write her biographical book and memoir, "Living The Big Sky Life," which was published in 2014.

DK was additionally honored to contribute the Foreword introduction to "The Galactic Transcripts," published in 2013 by her friend, numerologist and prolific author, Richard Andrew King.

www.LivingTheBigSkyLife.com
www.DKKing.com

"Living The Big Sky Life™" and "DK" logo are the trademarks of DK King and EmPress DK Publications.

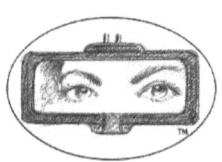

KAd Collins

KAd Collins is an intuitive visual artist who merges magical surrealism with her interest in celestial splendors by creating dreamlike compositions around the face using her extensive knowledge of symbolism to enhance the narrative.

Her etheric approach unveils a reverent focus on Starseed Beings who have lived lifetimes across galaxies, and the concepts around wandering soul families that are bridged between the worlds. Renown for her mesmerizing portraiture, KAd's surreal expressions of the divine spirit is beautifully reflected in each piece of art she creates.

KAd was honored to contribute the Artist's Perspective to "The Galactic Transcripts," published in 2013 by her friend, numerologist and prolific author, Richard Andrew King.

kacollinsartist@Instagram.com

DK KING
Books

www.LivingTheBigSkyLife.com,
Amazon.com and Major Online Retailers

"**Living The Big Sky Life**" is a clever memoir by DK King that will take you on a healing journey from the outside in - from the coastlines of Orange County, California, to the big sky resort town of Whitefish, Montana.

In a written voice that can be described as nothing short of audacious - real, raw and irreverent - DK King portrays her powerful passage through the peaks and valleys of love and life on her quintessential quest to turn the lemons in her life into an ocean of lemonade.

Recounting her personal ordeal with vivid clarity and unparalleled recall, DK King chronicles an unforgettable series of transformational experiences like only a great storyteller can. Her fearless account is truly captivating, and should be a must-read for anyone who dreams of exchanging their robust urban lifestyle for the simple life in any small town U.S.A.

This is a book you won't be able to put down until the startling end!

"Living The Big Sky Life™" and "DK" logo are the trademarks of DK King and EmPress DK Publications.

THE GALACTIC TRANSCRIPTS
By Richard Andrew King

www.TheGalacticTranscripts.com, RichardKing.net,
Amazon.com and Major Online Retailers

"The Galactic Transcripts" will take you on a journey that is as provocative as it is mysterious. Its thirty-seven transmissions are channeled from a non-earth, alien group who identify themselves as members of the Space Brotherhood.

"The Galactic Transcripts" offer us descriptions of other worlds, their inhabitants, morals, ethics, and histories. They even forewarn of the coming cleansing of earth and the cataclysms preceding it. Other messages shed light on the original colonization of earth, telepathic communication, the power of love, the program of the Radiant One, and much more.

Those who have read "The Galactic Transcripts" have found them to be life-altering, profound, inspirational, transformative. Will they have that effect on you? Open your mind and allow the transcripts to take you beyond the limitations of our world and into new, undiscovered worlds far beyond our galaxy.

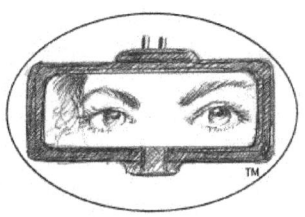

InTheRearViewMirror.com

www.ingramcontent.com/pod-product-compliance
Lightning Source LLC
Chambersburg PA
CBHW060505090426
42735CB00011B/2116